San Zi J...g
三字经

Three Character Classic
in Chinese and English

Pocket Edition

Written by Wang Yinglin
Translation and Commentary by Jeff Pepper

Book design by Jeff Pepper
Illustrations by Next Mars Media

IMAGIN8
PRESS

ISBN: 978-1952601316

ACKNOWLEDGMENTS

We are deeply indebted to the many scholars who have research, translated and commented on the San Zi Jing over the last eight centuries. We are especially grateful to Herbert Giles, whose translation published in 1900 has been accepted as the "gold standard" for over a century. There are also many excellent websites for researchers, please see the two Resources sections at the end of this book to learn more about them.

Many thanks to Lianghao Lu for his valuable assistance in reviewing the manuscript, and the team at Next Mars Media for their terrific illustrations.

Version 22

AUDIOBOOK

A complete Chinese language audio version of the San Zi Jing verses in this book is available free of charge. To access it, go to **www.youtube.com** and search for the Imagin8 Press channel. There you will find free audiobooks for this and many of our other books.

You can also visit our website, **www.imagin8press.com**, where you will find a direct link to the YouTube audiobook as well as information about our other books.

QR CODES

Throughout this book you'll see QR codes. These are pictures that your smartphone camera will convert to a web address. So for example in Section 3 verse 26 you'll see this QR code:

If you direct your smartphone camera to this code, it will convert the code to the web address **https://www.heredg.com/2015/12/the-end-of-the-song/,** which will take you to an interesting article about the end of the Song Dynasty.

The good news is that we use "static QR codes" which have no tracking software, so nobody will ever know whether you have used this code or not.

However, though we have tried to use high-quality websites for these codes, we have no control over the sites. The owners may delete or change the pages, so please don't be surprised if you get a "page not found" error or similar message from time to time.

INTRODUCTION

Welcome to 三字经, the San Zi Jing, known in English as the *Three Character Classic.* The Chinese character 三 is pronounced sān and, as you might guess from looking at it, means "the number three." The character 字 is pronounced zì and means "a written Chinese character." And the character 经 is pronounced jīng and means "a classic book."

The San Zi Jing was written by Wang Yinglin during the Song Dynasty in the 13th century, modified many times since then, and memorized by generations of Chinese students. It's a box of treasures, a puzzle within a puzzle, with layers of meaning waiting for you to discover.

At the simplest level, the San Zi Jing is just a workbook, a way for you to learn how to read, speak and write Chinese. The book consists of 101 verses. Each verse is a set of four phrases of three characters each, for a total of 12 characters. For example, the very first verse reads:

人之初，性本善。
性相近，习相远。

In pinyin, which is the phonetic spelling system used by foreigners and young Chinese kids and also used by everyone to type Chinese on a keyboard, this verse is:

Rén zhī chū, xìng běn shàn.
Xìng xiāng jìn, xí xiāng yuǎn.

Each character usually represents one word, so you can think of each verse as a twelve-word poem. But since Classical Chinese is a much more compact language than English, the English version is always longer than twelve words. This verse in English is translated as:

When people are born, their nature is good and all are alike.
But as they grow up and learn, they become different.

But the San Zi Jing is more than a workbook. It's is a grand tour of Chinese history. It starts off with brief stories about Confucian values and principles, then it shifts gears and takes us on a dizzying historical journey, starting with the legendary Yellow Emperor back in the misty beginnings of Chinese culture, and leading up to the end of the last dynasty in 1912. The verses are very short and extremely cryptic, so for each verse you'll see a short translation in contemporary English, and also a hundred words (exactly!) of commentary that we've written to help you understand the verse.

If you want to learn more, you can use the QR codes (see sample at right) at the bottom of each even-numbered page. Use your smartphone camera to visit these pages to find additional online  resources for each verse. If you want to read these but prefer not to use the QR code, the actual links are in the Resources for Learning section in the back.

And finally, the San Zi Jing is a window into the soul of China. Many of the verses provide bits of Confucian philosophy, or hint at stories told centuries ago. Even the historical verses in the middle of the book show us what life in China was like in the past, and give you a glimpse of how Chinese people see the world today. Read the San Zi Jing carefully, and you'll get a glimpse of what it's like to be Chinese.

A few quick notes before you dive in. The San Zi Jing is over 700 years old, and the Chinese language has evolved quite a bit since then. For that reason, reading the original text is similar to an American reading Beowulf or one of Shakespeare's plays today. Some of the words are unfamiliar even to educated modern Chinese speakers. Other words look the same but have changed meaning over the centuries. To make things even trickier, Chinese words often have many, many different possible meanings depending on context. So for each word in the verse you'll see a one-word translation that tells you what it means in that context when the book was written. That might not match how the word is used in ordinary conversation today.

To make things a bit easier for you, we use the Simplified Chinese character set that's standard in mainland China and around the world, rather than the original Traditional (or Complex) character set still used in Taiwan. So for example, the title of this book is written as 三字经 instead of 三字經. Same words, but somewhat simpler characters.

And finally, you'll notice that in pinyin most vowels have little marks called "tone marks" above them. So for example, the book's title in pinyin is Sān Zì Jīng. The tone marks tell you how to pronounce the word using the five different tones in modern Chinese: a high flat tone (ā), a rising tone (á), a down-and-up tone (ǎ), a falling tone (à), and a neutral tone (a). To hear the correct pronounciation of the words, listen to the free audiobook available on YouTube's Imagin8 Channel.

OK, let's get started!

Three Character Classic

三字经

Mencius's mother ripped the cloth from her weaving loom to show him how wasteful it was for him to neglect his studies.

- from Part 1, Verse 3

人之初，性本善。
性相近，习相远。

Rén zhī chū, xìng běn shàn.
Xìng xiāng jìn, xí xiāng yuǎn.

When people are born,
their nature is good and all are alike.
But as they grow up and learn, they become different.

人	rén	person
之	zhī	of ⇆
初	chū	early, at first
性	xìng	nature
本	běn	root, origin
善	shàn	good
性	xìng	nature
相	xiāng	appears
近	jìn	close
习	xí	learn
相	xiāng	appears
远	yuǎn	far

According to Confucius, when children are born they have no personality, and seem to be very similar to each other. But as they grow up, they change because of the influences of the world around them. This is why a child's education is so important. If a child does not receive a good education from a young age, their good nature will deteriorate. So, a child must study well from a young age, learning to tell good from evil, so they can grow up to be a useful member of society.

苟不教，性乃迁。
教之道，贵以专。

Gǒu bú jiào, xìng nǎi qiān.
Jiào zhī dào, guì yǐ zhuān.

Neglect the child's education, and their nature changes.
The right way to teach is with consistent focus.

苟	gǒu	if
不	bú	not
教	jiào	teach
性	xìng	nature
乃	nǎi	therefore
迁	qiān	change
教	jiào	teach
之	zhī	of 与
道	dào	path, way
贵	guì	most valuable
以	yǐ	using
专	zhuān	concentrate

Parents must always pay attention to the education of their children and never relax. If they neglect it, the bad side of human nature will prevail.

In ancient times, Zhou Chu grew up wild and often fought with others. One day the people of his village thought a tiger killed him and they celebrated. Zhou returned, saw this and immediately realized his mistake. An elder said to him, "learn wisdom in the morning, and it will be worthwhile to die at night." He changed his ways and went on to become a famous government official in the first Jin Dynasty.

昔孟母，择邻处。
子不学，断机杼。

Xī mèng mǔ, zé lín chǔ.
Zǐ bù xué, duàn jī zhù.

Long ago, Mencius's mother carefully chose new neighbors.
He did not learn, so she broke her loom.

昔	xī	past
孟	mèng	Mencius
母	mǔ	mother
择	zé	select
邻	lín	neighbor
处	chǔ	to live in
子	zi	child
不	bù	not
学	xué	learn
断	duàn	break
机	jī	machine, loom
杼	zhù	shuttle

Mencius (Men Ke) and his mother lived in a rustic mountain village, but she wanted a better learning environment for her gifted son. So when he was 3 years old she moved three times to find the best place to live. He started at a new school, but one day he skipped class. She ripped the cloth from her weaving loom to show him how wasteful it was for him to neglect his studies. He returned to school and eventually studied under Zisi, the grandson of Confucius. Mencius grew up to be the "Asian Saint," a great Confucian master.

14

窦燕山，有义方。
教五子，名俱扬。

Dòu yān shān, yǒu yì fāng,
Jiào wǔ zǐ, míng jù yáng.

Dou of Swallow Mountain had proper methods.
He taught five children,
and they all enhanced the family's reputation.

窦	dòu	Dou
燕	yān	Yan Shan
山	shān	
有	yǒu	have
义	yì	proper
方	fāng	method
教	jiāo	teach
五	wǔ	five
子	zǐ	child
名	míng	reputation
俱	jù	all
扬	yáng	spread far

Education is based on methods; you need the right methods to get the desired results.

Dou Yujun lived in Yanshan (Swallow Mountain). He was an orphan and a troublemaker. One night he dreamed his late grandfather told him, "Your karma is heavy, your life will be short. But change your ways and you may yet live!" He changed his life and was blessed with five sons. He taught them well. He lived to the age of 82 and died a happy man. His good deeds gave him a calm heart, positive attitude, good reputation, and long life.

养不教，父之过。
教不严，师之惰。

Yǎng bù jiào, fù zhī guò.
Jiāo bù yán, shī zhī duò.

Raising without teaching is the fault of the father.
Teaching without strictness is the laziness of the teacher.

养	yǎng	to raise, to feed
不	bù	without
教	jiào	teaching
父	fù	father
之	zhī	of ⇆ (see note)
过	guò	mistake, crime
教	jiào	to teach
不	bù	without
严	yán	strict, harsh
师	shī	teacher
之	zhī	of ⇆
惰	duò	lazy, careless

Strict education is the key to success. Children should understand the hard work of their parents and teachers. But parents must lead by doing, not just by talking.

Zeng Guofan was a famous courtier with many famous descendants. He showed his children how to lead a simple, hardworking life, avoiding rich foods and fine clothes. He showed them the importance of reading and learning. Anything that he asked of his children, he first demanded of himself. He was a father and a friend, and he won the respect and love of his children.

NOTE: when used in the middle of a phrase or sentence, 之 (zhī) means "of" but with the words before and after it reversed compared to English. So in this example, 父之过 means "mistake of the father."

子不学，非所宜。
幼不学，老何为。

Zǐ bù xué, fēi suǒ yí.
Yòu bù xué, lǎo hé wèi.

If a child does not learn, this is improper.
If you don't study when you are young,
what will you do when you are old?

子	zǐ	child
不	bù	not
学	xué	learn, study
非	fēi	not
所	suǒ	<for him>
宜	yí	suitable, proper
幼	yòu	child
不	bù	not
学	xué	learn, study
老	lǎo	old
何	hé	what
为	wèi	act

No matter who you are, you must study hard when you are young, so you will master the skills you need as an adult. Otherwise, when you become older you will not understand truth and you will have no knowledge.

Zhuang Bo was a poor student and had trouble learning, so he decided to write out his reading materials twenty times, but still he forgot the next morning. So he wrote it again and again, a hundred times over. Now he could remember and recite it perfectly.

17

玉不琢，不成器。
人不学，不知义。

Yù bù zhuó, bù chéng qì.
Rén bù xué, bù zhī yì.

Jade that is not polished is not a finished product.
A person who has not learned cannot know virtue.

玉	yù	jade
不	bù	not
琢	zuó	polish
不	bù	not
成	chéng	finish
器	qì	tool
人	rén	person
不	bù	not
学	xué	learn
不	bù	not
知	zhī	know
义	yì	morality

Zhuang Bo continued to work hard at his studies. He was like a piece of unfinished jade being polished. He would read an article, memorize it, burn the original, then write it from memory. He did this over and over again, until his hand was callused from writing. In the winter his skin froze and cracked. He would forget to eat, and relied on friends coming to bring him dumplings. Eventually he acquired profound knowledge and became a famous writer. His thoughts were quick, and his writing was fluent and profound.

为人子，方少时，
亲师友，习礼仪。

Wéi rén zǐ, fāng shào shí.
Qīn shī yǒu, xí lǐyí.

As your parent's child, when you are young,
Stay close to teachers and friends, learn proper behavior.

为	wèi	as
人	rén	person
子	zǐ	child
方	fāng	equal to
少	shǎo	young, small
时	shí	time
亲	qīn	dear, close
师	shī	teacher
友	yǒu	friend
习	xí	learn
礼	lǐ	etiquette, ceremonies
仪	yí	

We must learn from others, so remain close to your teachers and friends. Respect your teachers and your friends so they can pass on their knowledge to you.

Yang Shi was a learned man in the Song Dynasty. He had great respect for his teachers. One day he went with his friends to see his teacher Cheng Yi. The teacher was sleeping, so Yang Shi waited outside. It began to snow, but he would rather become buried in snow than disturb his teacher's nap.

"Snow Piles Up At Cheng Yi's Door" describes anyone with respect and reverence for their teacher.

香九龄，能温席。
孝于亲，所当执。

Xiāng jiǔ líng, néng wēn xí.
Xiào yú qīn, suǒ dāng zhí.

Xiang at age nine warmed his father's pillow.
Remain devoted and obedient to your parents.

香	xiāng	Xiang
九	jiǔ	nine
龄	líng	age
能	néng	could
温	wēn	warm
席	xí	pillow
孝	xiào	filial piety
于	yú	to
亲	qīn	parents
所	suǒ	what
当	dāng	proper
执	zhí	carry out

Respect for one's parents is the most important relationship in life. If you don't love and respect your parents, how can you love your country and its people?

Huang Xiang's mother died when he was nine. In summer he cooled his father's pillow by fanning it, in winter he warmed the pillow with his body heat before his father went to bed. At a young age he read the Confucian classics and wrote many articles. Later he became a senior official in the Eastern Han Dynasty. His story was told in the book, "The Twenty-Four Filial Sons" by Guo Shouzheng.

20

融四岁，能让梨。
弟于长，宜先知。

Róng sì suì, néng ràng lí.
Dì yú zhǎng, yí xiān zhī.

Rong at age four gave up his pears.
Respecting your elder brother
is the first thing you should know.

融	róng	Rong
四	sì	four
岁	suì	years old
能	néng	can
让	ràng	yield
梨	lí	pear
弟	dì	younger brother
于	yú	to
长	zhǎng	older brother
宜	yí	proper
先	xiān	first
知	zhī	to know

Honor and respect for one's siblings is also an important relationship. We should be willing to suffer losses for the sake of our brothers and sisters.

When Kong Rong was four years old, his father brought home some pears and handed him the largest. But Kong Rong shook his head and selected the smallest one, saying "I am younger, so I should eat the smaller pears than my older brothers." "But what about your younger brother?" asked his father. "I am older than him, so I should leave the bigger one to him." Later, Kong Rong became a famous statesman.

21

首孝弟，次见闻。
知某数，识某文。

Shǒu xiào tì, cì jiànwén.
Zhī mǒu shù, shí mǒu wén.

First is filial piety, then learn to look and listen.
Learn to count, learn to read.

首	shǒu	first
孝	xiào	filial piety
弟	tì	
次	cì	next
见	jiàn	what one sees and hears, information
闻	wén	
知	zhī	know
某	mǒu	certain
数	shù	number
识	shí	knowledge
某	mǒu	certain
文	wén	language

First learn to respect your parents and siblings, then master what you see and hear.

The four Wu brothers were born in a very poor family, their parents had to sell them to a rich family as child servants. They worked hard, saved their money, and returned home to care for their elderly parents. At first they took turns, each one serving one month out of four. Then they served one day out of four. On the fifth day, they always gathered for a big family meal. The parents lived to be a hundred and died in peace.

一而十，十而百，
百而千，千而万。

Yī ér shí, shí ér bǎi,
bǎi ér qiān, qiān ér wàn.

One to ten, ten to a hundred,
A hundred to a thousand, a thousand to ten thousand.

一	yī	one
而	ér	and, then
十	shí	ten
十	shí	ten
而	ér	and, then
百	bǎi	hundred
百	bǎi	hundred
而	ér	and, then
千	qiān	thousand
千	qiān	thousand
而	ér	and, then
万	wàn	ten thousand

It's important to learn basic arithmetic and advanced mathematics, not just literature and philosophy. Every aspect of science is based on mathematics, so this is the foundation of all other scientific knowledge. Counting from one to ten is easy, but the possibilities of mathematics are endless. The ancient Chinese used counting tools such as jade shells, knotted ropes, and the abacus. The earliest form of writing in China, oracle bones, had symbols for numbers, and those can still be seen today in modern Chinese characters.

三才者，天地人。
三光者，日月星。

Sān cái zhě, tiān dì rén.
Sān guāng zhě, rì yuè xīng.

The three forces are: heaven, earth and humanity.
The three lights are: sun, moon and stars.

三	sān	three
才	cái	talent, ability
者	zhě	\<it is\>
天	tiān	heaven
地	dì	earth
人	rén	person
三	sān	three
光	guāng	light
者	zhě	\<it is\>
日	rì	sun
月	yuè	moon
星	xīng	star

The universe is vast, consisting of heaven above, earth below, and humanity in the middle. The sun, moon and stars bring light and warmth to everything on earth. We must show courage and expand our knowledge beyond the small circles around us.

In the 14th century Ming Dynasty, the scholar Wan Hu dreamed of rising from earth to heaven. He tied 47 homemade rockets to a chair, sat in the chair, and lit the rockets. They exploded and he died. But recently a crater on the moon was named in his honor. His dream of conquering the sky lives on.

三纲者，君臣义，
父子亲，夫妇顺。

Sān gāng zhě, jūn chén yì,
fù zǐ qīn, fū fù shùn.

The three principles are: duty between ruler and subject,
Love between father and child,
harmony between husband and wife.

三	sān	three
纲	gāng	principles
者	zhě	\<it is\>
君	jūn	ruler
臣	chén	subject
义	yì	righteousness
父	fù	father
子	zǐ	child
亲	qīn	closeness
夫	fū	husband
妇	fù	wife
顺	shùn	obedience, harmony

Chinese culture is based on rules for living in harmony.

A doctor named Chun Yuyi treated the wife of a powerful man, but the wife died. The man reported him and Chun was arrested and sent to Chang'an for punishment. His daughter Xiao would not leave him. When they arrived at Chang'an, she sent a letter to the emperor, saying that if her father were crippled, he could not improve himself afterwards or contribute to society.

The emperor agreed, and so he banned corporal punishment. Xiao saved her father and many others. This is why filial piety is so important.

曰春夏，曰秋冬，
此四时，运不穷。

Yuē chūn xià, yuē qiū dōng,
cǐ sì shí, yùn bù qióng.

Speak of spring and summer, autumn and winter,
These four seasons revolve without end.

曰	yuē	speak
春	chūn	spring
夏	xià	summer
曰	yuē	speak
秋	qiū	autumn
冬	dōng	winter
此	cǐ	these
四	sì	four
时	shí	seasons
运	yùn	migrate
不	bù	not
穷	qióng	end

The seasons arise from the tilt of the earth as it rotates, as we face the sun directly in summer and at an angle in winter. But long ago, the people believed in Zhu Long, the Torch Dragon, who lives in a magical mountain beyond the Chushui River. It is said that he creates the seasons, breathing in to bring summer and breathing out to bring winter. Morning comes when he opens his eyes, and night when he closes them. He does not eat or drink, he just rests beneath the mountain, bringing rain and wind with his fiery breath.

曰南北，曰西东，
此四方，应乎中。

Yuē nán běi, yuē xī dōng,
cǐ sì fāng, yìng hū zhōng.

Speak of south and north, of west and east,
These four directions arise from the center.

曰	yuē	speak
南	nán	south
北	běi	north
曰	yuē	speak
西	xī	west
东	dōng	east
此	cǐ	these
四	sì	four
方	fāng	directions
应	yìng	correspond
乎	hū	from
中	zhōng	center

There are four points on the compass, and each direction comes from a central point. People also need a strong sense of direction to avoid becoming lost and confused.

Chiyou was an tribal chieftan in ancient China who, with his 81 brothers, fought against the legendary Yellow Emperor. Chiyou was winning the battle when a dense fog blanketed the battlefield. He could not tell where the enemy was, so he withdrew his soldiers. But the emperor had a newly invented device, an iron compass, mounted on his chariot. Relying on the compass, the Yellow Emperor defeated Chiyou's army.

曰水火，木金土，
此五行，本乎数。

Yuē shuǐ huǒ, mù jīn tǔ,
cǐ wǔ xíng, běn hū shù.

Speak of water, fire, wood, metal and earth,
These five elements are rooted in numbers.

曰	yuē	speak
水	shuǐ	water
火	huǒ	fire
木	mù	wood
金	jīn	metal, gold
土	tǔ	earth
此	cǐ	these
五	wǔ	five
行	xíng	elements
本	běn	root
乎	hū	in
数	shù	mathematical order

Five elements make up all matter. They interact: water to fire, fire to metal, metal to wood, wood to earth, and earth to water. These interactions are governed by mathematics, and the five elements spring from numerical order.

Da Yu was ordered by the emperor to find a way to control annual floods which killed many people. Yu studied the problem carefully, and realized that water could wash away earth, but earth could hold back water. He and his workers spent thirteen years digging channels and building levees. Finally, flooding was controlled and the people lived in peace and harmony.

曰仁义，礼智信，
此五常，不容紊。

Yuē rén yì, lǐ zhì xìn,
cǐ wǔ cháng, bù róng wěn.

Speak of kindness, duty, courtesy, wisdom and truth,
These five constants must not be compromised.

曰	yuē	speak
仁	rén	humaneness
义	yì	right conduct
礼	lǐ	courtesy
智	zhì	wisdom
信	xìn	faith, honesty
此	cǐ	these
五	wǔ	five
常	cháng	virtues
不	bù	not
容	róng	tolerate
紊	wěn	to change

These five moral principles are the core of Confucianism, just as important today as in ancient times. If everyone is treated with courtesy and kindness, society will be peaceful and harmonious.

The first king of Wei made plans to go hunting with the man who managed his forest. But a huge storm came and the king could not go. One of his ministers prepared to tell the forester, but the king stopped him, saying "I will go myself." The ministers thought the king was being foolish, but the king understood the importance of treating everyone according to these five principles.

稻粱菽，麦黍稷，
此六谷，人所食。

Dào liáng shū, mài shǔ jì,
cǐ liù gǔ, rén suǒ shí.

Rice, sorghum, beans, wheat, sticky millet, common millet,
These six grains are what people eat.

稻	dào	rice
粱	liáng	sorghum
菽	shū	beans
麦	mài	wheat
黍	shǔ	sticky millet
稷	jì	common millet
此	cǐ	these
六	liù	six
谷	gǔ	grain
人	rén	people
所	suǒ	which
食	shí	eat, food

We eat these foods every day, but do we cherish them, and think of those who grow and prepare them?

Chen Yi's mother never wasted food. She even served guoba, the crispy layer of burned rice scraped from the bottom of a pot, saying, "This is fragrant, eat it!" When he was older, Yi was a commander in the army. His troops lost a battle and had to hide in the woods. They were hungry. Yi thought of their cooking pots and the burned food stuck to the bottom. He retrieved the pots and the men survived until rescue came.

马牛羊，鸡犬豕，
此六畜，人所饲。

Mǎ niú yáng, jī quǎn shǐ,
cǐ liù chù, rén suǒ sì.

Horse, cow, sheep, chicken, dog, pig,
These six animals are what people raise.

马	mǎ	horse
牛	niú	cow
羊	yáng	sheep
鸡	jī	chicken
犬	quǎn	dog
豕	shǐ	hog
此	cǐ	these
六	liù	six
畜	chù	livestock
人	rén	people
所	suǒ	which
饲	sì	breed

These are the six main domesticated animals.

According to legend, Fuxi learned long ago to tame wild animals for his own use. Before that, people lived by hunting wild animals and gathering wild food, but in bad weather the people would go hungry. So Fuxi taught them how to catch the wild animals and keep them in reserve. Later, they learned to select the ones with the most desireable traits and breed them.

The six types of animals are used for food, but they also perform many useful tasks, and they provide us with companionship.

曰喜怒，曰哀惧，
爱恶欲，七情具。

Yuē xǐ nù, yuē āi jù,
ài wù yù, qī qíng jù.

Speak of joy and anger, speak of sadness and fear,
Love, hate and desire, these are the seven emotions.

曰	yuē	speak
喜	xǐ	to like
怒	nù	anger, rage
曰	yuē	speak
哀	āi	sadness, grief
惧	jù	fear
爱	ài	love
恶	wù	hate, loathe
欲	yù	desire, appetite
七	qī	seven
情	qíng	emotion
具	jù	to list

We are all born with these seven emotions, and we must learn to manage our feelings to have a happy and meaningful life. But we can't simply ignore our feelings either.

Du Zichun, a wealthy young man, wasted all his family's money and became a street beggar. A Taoist priest told him, "Sit in complete silence for one night, and you will become immortal." That night Du dreamed that he lived an entire life filled with the seven emotions. Just as dawn was breaking, in his dream his child was killed. Du cried out and thus failed the priest's test.

匏土革，木石金，
与丝竹，乃八音。

Páo tǔ gé, mù shí jīn,
yǔ sī zhú, nǎi bā yīn.

Gourd, clay, leather, wood, stone and metal,
Also silk and bamboo, these give the eight sounds.

匏	páo	gourd
土	tǔ	clay
革	gé	leather
木	mù	wood
石	shí	stone
金	jīn	metal
与	yǔ	together with
丝	sī	silk, string
竹	zhú	bamboo
乃	nǎi	thus
八	bā	eight
音	yīn	sound

Over seventy traditional Chinese instruments are made from these eight materials. The materials make the instruments, but music comes from the sounds of nature combined with our appreciation and understanding.

Boya studied the guqin but his teacher felt he lacked a deep understanding. "Let's go see my teacher," said the teacher. They arrived on an island. The teacher told Boya to wait and practice the guqin. Every day he played while listening to the sounds of the sea and forest. Ten days later his teacher returned and said, "You are now the best player in the world. Let's go home."

高曾祖，父而身，
身而子，子而孙。

Gāo zēng zǔ, fù ér shēn,
shēn ér zǐ, zǐ ér sūn.

Great great grandfather to great grandfather,
to grandfather, to father, to me,
Me to my son, son to grandson.

高	gāo	great great grandfather
曾	zēng	great grandfather
祖	zǔ	grandfather
父	fù	father
而	ér	to
身	shēn	oneself
身	shēn	oneself
而	ér	to
子	zǐ	son
子	zǐ	son
而	ér	to
孙	sūn	grandson

Water has its source, trees have their roots, and we all come from those before us. We bear the responsibilities of our ancestors, and will be the ancestors of those who follow us.

In the Han Dynasty, the mother of Wei, a young scholar, hit him with a stick whenever he made a mistake. He never complained, but one day he cried after being hit. Worried, his mother asked if she hit him too hard. He replied, "No, you usually hit me very hard. Today you hit me lightly, so I'm worried that perhaps you are not in good health."

自子孙，至玄曾，
乃九族，人之伦。

Zì zǐsūn, zhì xuán zēng,
nǎi jiǔzú, rén zhī lún.

From son and grandson to great-great-grandson,
These nine generations are the kinships of people.

自	zì	from
子	zǐ	son
孙	sūn	grandson
至	zhì	to
玄	xuán	great great grandson
曾	zēng	great grandson
乃	nǎi	these
九	jiǔ	nine
族	zú	generations
人	rén	people
之	zhī	of ⇆
伦	lún	relationship, order

A person counts four generations upwards: father, grandfather, great grandfather, and great great grandfather, then four generations downward: son, grandson, great grandson, and great great grandson. These are the nine generations, the inherited relationships of the family line.

Bo Qin asked his father the same question many times. Each time the father refused to answer. Puzzled, Bo asked a wise merchant why. The merchant pointed to two trees, saying, "That tree is tall and straight, but that one is low and inferior. Think about these two trees carefully, and you'll know why." Bo realized he had forgotten respect and humility.

父子恩，夫妇从，
兄则友，弟则恭。

Fù zǐ ēn, fū fù cóng,
xiōng zé yǒu, dì zé gōng.

Kindness between father and son,
harmony between husband and wife,
Friendship from older brothers,
respect from younger brothers.

父	fù	father
子	zǐ	son
恩	ēn	kindness
夫	fū	husband
妇	fù	wife
从	cóng	harmony
兄	xiōng	older brother
则	zé	then
友	yǒu	friendship
弟	dì	younger brother
则	zé	then
恭	gōng	respect

Family members should treat each other politely, provide friendship and support, and live in harmony. Family is the core of society. If the family is in harmony, the society is stable.

Xiao and Li were brothers during the Han Dynasty. One day, hungry robbers broke into their house. They saw Li and decided to eat him, but Xiao knelt before them and said, "Honored guests, eat me instead, my meat is more tasty." Although the robbers were hungry, this changed their hearts. They took a few things and left the house without harming either brother.

长幼序，友与朋，
君则敬，臣则忠。

Zhǎng yòu xù, yǒu yǔ péng,
jūn zé jìng, chén zé zhōng.

Order between elders and youngsters,
friendship between friends,
Respect from rulers, loyalty from subjects.

长	zhǎng	older
幼	yòu	younger
序	xù	rank order
友	yǒu	friend
与	yǔ	together with
朋	péng	friend
君	jūn	lord, sovereign
则	zé	then
敬	jìng	respect
臣	chén	subject
则	zé	then
忠	zhōng	loyal

The Chinese have always paid great attention to obeying the rules of living with others. These guide the interactions of older and younger people, of friends with each other, of rulers towards their subjects, and subjects towards their rulers.

Zhang Qu and his friend studied together at Luoyang. When school ended his friend said, "Don't be sad, I will visit your home in two years." Two years later, Zhang heard geese calling, and rushed home to tell his mother his friend was coming. "He is a trustworthy friend, he will come." And sure enough, the friend arrived exactly on time.

此十义，人所同。
当师叙, 勿违背。

Cǐ shí yì, rén suǒ tóng.
Dāng shī xù, wù wéi bèi.

These ten obligations are the same for all.
Follow instructions, don't argue back.

此	cǐ	these
十	shí	ten
义	yì	obligations
人	rén	people
所	suǒ	actually
同	tóng	same
当	dāng	should
师	shī	obey
叙	xù	order
勿	wù	don't
违	wéi	disobey
背	bèi	back

The ten obligations of Confucianism are: kindness between father and child, harmony between husband and wife, friendship from older siblings, respect from younger siblings, order between older and younger, respect from rulers, and loyalty from subjects. The ancient Chinese saying is, "The family is strong, and so the state is stable."

An eight year old boy in the Jin Dynasty was so poor that his family could not afford mosquito nets. To protect his parents from bites, he sat naked on his bed after they went to sleep, so the mosquitos would drink blood from him instead of his parents.

Part 2

The boss paid him much less than he expected!

- from Part 2, Verse 1

凡训蒙，须讲究。
详训诂，明句读。

Fán xùn méng, xū jiǎng jiū.
Xiáng xùngǔ, míng jù dòu.

When teaching new students, you must explain clearly.
Teach the ancient texts,
show how to identify sentences and punctuation.

凡	fán	every
训	xùn	teach
蒙	méng	new student
须	xū	must
讲	jiǎng	explain
究	jiū	thoroughly
详	xiáng	detailed
训	xùn	explain the
诂	gǔ	ancient texts
明	míng	understand
句	jù	sentence
读	dòu	punctuation

A child starting school had to learn to read and write each character, using the classic texts. But ancient written Chinese had no punctuation, so to avoid confusion students had to learn to recognize breaks in phrases, sentences and paragraphs.

A wealthy but stingy man once hired a new cook and wrote these instructions for meals: "No chicken duck fish. Don't forget vegetables and wine." Later when the cook resigned, he asked to be repaid for his expenses. The boss read it as "No chicken duck fish don't. Forget vegetables and wine." The cook got much less than he expected!

40

为学者，必有初。
小学终，至四书。

Wéi xué zhě, bì yǒu chū.
Xiǎo xué zhōng, zhì sìshū.

Those who study surely must have a beginning.
Basic schooling finished, they move on to the Four Classics.

为	wèi	in the role of
学	xué	study
者	zhě	<it is>
必	bì	surely
有	yǒu	have
初	chū	beginning
小	xiǎo	small
学	xué	elementary learning
终	zhōng	finish
至	zhì	arrive
四	sì	Four Classics
书	shū	

Students must start with a good educational foundation. But when primary school is finished, they next should study the Four Confucian Classics (sìshū). These were the core of the main curriculum for civil service exams in the Ming and Qing Dynasties. Great Learning is a chapter by Confucius plus nine commentary chapters by his disciple Zengzi. Doctrine of the Mean is by Confucius' grandson Zisi and shows how to gain perfect virtue. Analects is a set of speeches by Confucius and his disciples. And Mencius is a collection of detailed conversations between Mencius and various rulers of the Warring States.

论语者，二十篇。
群弟子，记善言。

Lúnyǔ zhě, èrshí piān;
Qún dìzǐ, jì shàn yán.

The Analects has twenty chapters.
Disciples have recorded the wise sayings of Confucius.

论	lún	Analects
语	yǔ	
者	zhě	<it is>
二	èr	twenty
十	shí	
篇	piān	chapter
群	qún	group
弟	dì	disciple
子	zǐ	
记	jì	remember
善	shàn	good
言	yán	words

The Analects contain the wisdom of Confucius. One day Confucius heard two of his students arguing. One of them asked him, "Master, what can I do to stop arguing all the time?" Confucius asked, "How many teeth do you have, and how many tongues?" "Thirty two, and one." "And what about that old man over there?" "None, and one." "Teeth are hard and strong and hurt the tongue many times. The tongue is peaceful and gentle, it helps the teeth and never hurts them. But as you see, the tongue endures while the teeth do not. Which one are you?"

孟子者，七篇止，
讲道德，说仁义。

Mèngzǐ zhě, qī piān zhǐ,
jiǎng dào dé, shuō rén yì.

The writings of Mencius, just seven chapters,
Explain the way of virtue
and speak of benevolence and righteousness.

孟	mèng	Mencius
子	zǐ	
者	zhě	\<it is\>
七	qī	seven
篇	piān	chapters
止	zhǐ	only
讲	jiǎng	explain
道	dào	path
德	dé	virtue
说	shuō	speaks
仁	rén	benevolence
义	yì	righteousness

Mencius lived four generations after Confucius and is considered second only to Confucius himself. He spoke often with kings and princes of the Warring States. He counseled them to cultivate moral power and give up the ways of force. He said, "the people are the most important element in a nation; the spirits of the land and grain come next; the sovereign counts for the least." He advocated for the common people and for democratic government. But he could not find any king willing to practice his ideas, so he retired to his home in Zou and focused on teaching.

作中庸，子思笔；
中不偏，庸不易。

Zuò zhōngyōng, zisī bǐ;
zhōng bù piān, yōng bù yì.

The Doctrine of the Mean, by the pen of Zisi;
The center does not tilt, the course does not change.

作	zuò	make
中	zhōng	Doctrine of the Mean
庸	yōng	
子	zi	Zisi
思	sī	
笔	bǐ	to write
中	zhōng	center
不	bù	not
偏	piān	lean
庸	yōng	course
不	bù	not
易	yì	change

Zisi, the only grandson of Confucius, wrote Doctrine of the Mean (zhōngyōng), which became required reading for generations of Chinese students. The goal of the mean (zhōng) is to achieve balance and harmony, maintain one's course (yōng), keep the mind in equilibrium, and remain on the path of duty.

It offers three main guidelines. First is self watchfulness: "The superior person is watchful over himself even when alone." Second is leniency: "What you do not like when done to yourself, do not do to others." Third is sincerity: "Give full development to the nature of other men, animals and things."

作大学，乃曾子。
自修齐，至平治

Zuò dàxué, nǎi zēngzǐ.
Zì xiū qí, zhì píng zhì.

The author of The Great Learning was Zengzi.
Cultivate the self, bring peace to the world,
govern the state.

作	zuò	make
大	dà	Great
学	xué	Learning
乃	nǎi	it was
曾	zēng	Zengzi
子	zǐ	
自	zì	self
修	xiū	self-cultivate
齐	qí	together
至	zhì	reach
平	píng	peaceful
治	zhì	rule

Zéng Shēn (also called Zéngzi) was 46 years younger than his teacher Confucius. He is considered one of the Four Sages of Confucianism. He wrote ten books, established his own school, and taught Confucius' grandson Zisi.

In The Great Learning (dàxué) he emphasized achieving balance in all things, bringing one's affairs into order and harmony, and encouraging learning and self-cultivation. He taught that through self-cultivation one can bring order and harmony to one's mind, personal life, family, state and the world as a whole. But he emphasized that his teachings applied to all people, not just rulers and scholars.

孝经通，四书熟，
如六经，始可读。

Xiàojīng tōng, sì shū shú,
rú liù jīng, shǐ kě dú.

Master the Classic of Filial Piety, learn the Four Books,
Then you can begin studying the Six Classics.

孝	xiào	Classic of Filial Piety
经	jīng	
通	tōng	know well
四	sì	four
书	shū	books
熟	shú	familiar
如	rú	such as
六	liù	six
经	jīng	classics
始	shǐ	begin
可	kě	can
读	dú	read

One should master the Four Books and understand filial piety (xiào) before reading the Six (now only five) Classics. The Classic of Filial Piety is a conversation between Confucius and his student Zengzi on how to establish a peaceful society based on this principle.

Yu Chonghua's father and stepbrothers tried to kill him many times. He fixed a barn roof, they set it on fire. He dug a well, they tried to collapse it. But still he showed no jealousy and remained obedient to his father and kind to his brothers. The Emperor was pleased, and made Chonghua his heir.

诗书易，礼春秋，
号六经，当讲求。

Shī shū yì, lǐ chūn qiū,
hào liù jīng, dāng jiǎng qiú.

The Books of Poetry, Documents and Changes,
The Rites of Zhou, The Book of Rites,
The Spring and Autumn Annals,
These are the Six Classics
which should be discussed and analyzed.

诗	shī	poem, song
书	shū	document
易	yì	change
礼	lǐ	rites
春	chūn	spring
秋	qiū	autumn
号	hào	number
六	liù	six
经	jīng	classics
当	dāng	should
讲	jiǎng	explain
求	qiú	seek

After mastering the Four Books and understanding filial piety, one can move on to study the next set of classics. We know of only five classic books: the Book of Changes (the I-Ching), the Book of Documents, the Book of Songs, the Book of Rites, and the Spring and Autumn Annals. The sixth, the Book of Music, has vanished without a trace.

These were written in ink on thin bamboo slips before the invention of paper in 105 A.D. Civil service applicants had to master these books, along with the Four Books, to pass the civil examination in ancient China.

有连山，有归藏，
有周易，三易详。

Yǒu lián shān, yǒu guī cáng,
yǒu zhōuyì, sān yì xiáng.

There is Lian Shan, there is Gui Cang,
There is Zhou Yi, these are the three books of changes.

有	yǒu	have
连	lián	
山	shān	Lian Shan
有	yǒu	have
归	guī	
藏	cáng	Gui Cang
有	yǒu	have
周	zhōu	
易	yì	Zhou Yi
三	sān	three
易	yì	changes
详	xiáng	complete

Three main books for telling the future were used in ancient China. The best known is the Book of Changes (zhōu yì), called I Ching in English. Its has 64 hexagrams, which are all possible combinations of six stacked horizontal lines with each line solid or broken. Each hexagram represents a concept. For example, the first six hexagrams stand for Creative, Receptive, Difficult, Folly, Waiting, and Conflict.

Someone "casts" the I Ching by sorting yarrow stalks or tossing six coins to select each hexagram. These are interpreted to predict the future, explain the present, or suggest a course of action.

有典谟，有训诰，
有誓命，书之奥。

Yǒu diǎn mó, yǒu xùn gào,
yǒu shì mìng, shū zhī ào.

There are regulations and consultations,
there are instructions and announcements,
there are declarations and commands,
these are the mysteries of the Book of Documents.

有	yǒu	have
典	diǎn	regulations
谟	mó	consultations
有	yǒu	have
训	xùn	admonishments
诰	gào	announcements
有	yǒu	have
誓	shì	declarations
命	mìng	commands
书	shū	Book of Documents
之	zhī	of ⇆
奥	ào	mystery

The Book of Documents (shū jīng) is an ancient document compiled by Confucius himself from several older works. Most of the book consists of formal speeches by kings and other leaders. It has six parts: Regulations (diǎn) with speeches by Emperors Yao and Shun, Consultations (mó) between the king and his ministers, Instructions (xùn) to the king from his ministers, Announcements (gào) by the king to his people, Declarations (shì) by the king during war, and Commands (mìng) by the king to his subjects.

我周公，作周礼，
著六官，存治体。

Wǒ zhōu gōng, zuò zhōu lǐ,
zhù liù guān, cún zhì tǐ.

Our Duke of Zhou wrote the Rites of Zhou,
Describing the six types of officials,
giving form to the government.

我	wǒ	my
周	zhōu	Zhou
公	gōng	duke
作	zuò	made
周	zhōu	Rites of Zhou
礼	lǐ	
著	zhù	make known
六	liù	six
官	guān	officials
存	cún	preserve
治	zhì	rule
体	tǐ	system

The six offices described in the Rites of Zhou are: Heaven (prime minister), Earth (taxation and land), Spring (education and religion), Summer (military), Autumn (justice), and Winter (public works).

The Duke of Zhou was the fourth son of King Wen and a talented regent for his young nephew King Cheng. He was so polite that if a visitor came to see him during his meal, he would spit out his food and run to meet them. He organized the government into six parts, and described in detail the roles of each. He also included guidelines for educating women.

大小戴，注礼记，
述圣言，礼乐备。

Dà xiǎo dài, zhù lǐ jì,
shù shèng yán, lǐ yuè bèi.

Older and Younger Dai explained the Book of Rites.
They told us the words of the sages,
so we can know the rites and music.

大	dà	big
小	xiǎo	small
戴	dài	Dai
注	zhù	explain
礼	lǐ	Book of Rites
记	jì	
述	shù	tell
圣	shèng	sage
言	yán	words
礼	lǐ	rites
乐	lè	music
备	bèi	ready, prepared

Dai the Greater (dà dài) and his nephew Dai the Lesser (xiǎo dài) were Confucian scholars during the reign of Emperor Yuan of the Former Han Dynasty. They edited the Book of Rites (lǐ jì), reorganizing and trimming it.

Confucius emphasized the principle of lǐ, which translates to English as rites, ceremonies, politeness, or rules of conduct. It is a system of piety and respect for others through traditional ritual, a stabilizing influence in changing times. He wrote, "Of all things to which the people owe their lives, lǐ is the most important."

曰国风，曰雅颂，
号四诗，当讽咏。

Yuē guó fēng, yuē yǎ sòng,
hào sì shī, dāng fěng yǒng.

Speak of Airs of the States, the Minor and Major Odes,
These four parts of the Book of Songs
should be recited and sung.

曰	yuē	speak
国	guó	state
风	fēng	wind
曰	yuē	speak
雅	yǎ	ode
颂	sòng	song
号	hào	number
四	sì	four
诗	shī	poem, song
当	dāng	should
讽	fěng	recite
咏	yǒng	sing

The Book of Songs, one of the Classic Books, contains over 300 poems. Its four sections are: Airs of the State (guó fēng), Minor and Major Odes (yǎ), and Songs (sòng). It is China's oldest collection of poems, some over 3,000 years old.

In one poem, Blue-Collared Lad (zǐ jǐn), a girl laments being ignored by her boyfriend, a young scholar in traditional blue robes. "Blue collared lad, you've long been in my heart, you're in my loving thoughts. I keep pacing and climbing the lookout tower. A day without seeing you is like three months!"

诗既亡，春秋作。
寓褒贬，别善恶。

Shī jì wáng, chūnqiū zuò,
Yù bāo biǎn, bié shàn è.

When the Book of Songs perished,
the Spring and Autumn Annals were made.
The Annals assigned praise and blame,
and told good from bad.

诗	shī	poem, song
既	jì	already
亡	wáng	perish
春	chūn	spring
秋	qiū	autumn
作	zuò	make
寓	yù	imply
褒	bāo	praise
贬	biǎn	criticism
别	bié	separate
善	shàn	good
恶	è	evil

The importance of the Book of Songs faded when the Zhou Dynasty collapsed, so Confucius wrote Spring and Autumn Annals during the Warring States period that followed, when China was split into dozens of small kingdoms.

The Annals originally were a list of brief notes averaging just 10 characters each on marriages, deaths, funerals, battles, natural disasters, and so on, but Confucius himself added his insightful commentaries. He assigned praise and blame to leaders, and discussed their good and evil behavior.

Since "Spring and Autumn" means the passage of a year, the book's title could be translated as "Yearly Records."

三传者，有公羊，
有左氏，有穀梁。

Sān zhuàn zhě, yǒu gōng yáng,
yǒu zuǒ shì, yǒu gǔ liáng.

There are three commentaries, from Gong Yang,
From Zuo, and from Gou Liang.

三	sān	three
传	zhuàn	commentaries
者	zhě	\<it is\>
有	yǒu	have
公	gōng	Gong Yang
羊	yáng	
有	yǒu	have
左	zuǒ	Zuo
氏	shì	name
有	yǒu	have
穀	gòu	Gou Liang
梁	liáng	

The Spring and Autumn Annals were very brief, so several scholars wrote commentaries to expand and explain them. The Commentary of Zuo, Commentary of Gongyang and Commentary of Guliang have all survived to the present day, others have disappeared.

One example of an Annals entry is: "Summer May, Zheng Bo defeated Duan at Yan." The real story is much more complicated, involving a king and queen, two sons competing for the throne, and one son's uncle who attacked the chosen son only to be defeated and driven away to Yan. Zuo's commentary brought this complex story to life.

经既明，方读子。
撮其要，记其事。

Jīng jì míng, fāng dú zǐ.
Cuō qí yào, jì qí shì.

When the classics are understood, read the philosophers.
Pick out their main points, and remember their facts.

经	jīng	classics
既	jì	already
明	míng	clear
方	fāng	then
读	dú	read
子	zǐ	respected men
撮	cuō	select
其	qí	their
要	yào	main point
记	jì	remember
其	qí	their
事	shì	affairs

Philosophers can give us new insights into everyday matters.

Confucius lived in the state of Lu, which rewarded those who paid ransom to free Lu citizens from slavery in other states. One of his students, Zi Gong, paid a ransom and freed several Lu citizens who were slaves. The Lu government tried to reward Zi Gong, but he refused the reward.

Confucius criticized him, saying that his action would shame others into not accepting rewards, this would discourage people from freeing slaves, and thus slavery would increase. So although his actions benefited him, it did great harm to society.

五子者，有荀扬，
文中子，及老庄。

Wǔzǐ zhě, yǒu xún yáng,
wénzhōng zǐ, jí lǎo zhuāng.

The five philosophers are Xunzi, Yangzi,
Wen Zhongzi, Laozi, and Zhuangzi.

五	wǔ	five
子	zǐ	\<title of respect>
者	zhě	\<it is>
有	yǒu	have
荀	xún	Xunzi
扬	yáng	Yangzi
文	wén	Wen Zhongzi
中	zhōng	
子	zǐ	
及	jí	and
老	lǎo	Laozi
庄	zhuāng	Zhuangzi

Xunzi (Xun Kuang) was a Confucian who claimed that moral rules are needed to keep people from following their inborn evil tendencies.

Yangzi (Yang Zhu) was a Daoist who believed that if people simply live in harmony with nature and avoid harming others, the world take care of itself.

Wen Zhongzi is actually the name of a book written by Wang Tong, a Confucian who developed a political system that showed how the Zhou, a foreign dynasty, could effectively rule China.

And Laozi (Lao Tzu) and Zhuangzi (Chuang Tzu) are the two most famous and influential philosophers of Daoism.

Part 3

Zhao presented Er Shi with a deer but called it a horse.

- from Part 3, Verse 10

经子通，读诸史，
考世系，知终始。

Jīngzǐ tōng, dú zhū shǐ,
kǎo shì xì, zhī zhōng shǐ.

Learn the classics, read the histories,
See the connections between eras,
know the ends and beginnings.

经	jīng	classics
子	zǐ	
通	tōng	know well
读	dú	read
诸	zhū	the many
史	shǐ	history
考	kǎo	examine
世	shì	era
系	xì	genealogy
知	zhī	know
终	zhōng	end
始	shǐ	beginning

Studying history is easy, but understanding it is a challenge. Try to see why one dynasty ends and another begins, and the reasons behind their rise and fall.

Usually when a new dynasty comes to power it gives lands to the peasants, reduces taxes, and eliminates corruption. Over time, though, emperors lose touch with the people, corruption increases, and rebellions start in the outer provinces. Eventually there is a major disaster or crisis that the emperor can't handle. Then powerful families rise up, the dynasty is overthrown, a new one takes power, and the cycle repeats.

自羲农，至黄帝，
号三皇，居上世。

Zì xī nóng, zhì huángdì,
hào sān huáng, jū shàng shì.

From Xi and Nong, to the Yellow Emperor,
These three emperors live on forever.

自	zì	from
羲	xī	Xi
农	nóng	Nong
至	zhì	to
黄	huáng	yellow
帝	dì	emperor
号	hào	count
三	sān	three
皇	huáng	emperors
居	jū	live
上	shàng	on
世	shì	forever

These three great emperors lived long ago, between 2953 BC and 2599 BC.

Fu Xi taught his subjects how to raise the "six animals": cattle, sheep, horses, pigs, chickens and dogs. He also taught them to fish using nets.

Shen Nong taught his people how to raise crops and also discovered medical uses for herbs and plants.

And the greatest of all, the Yellow Emperor, was a master of technology. Along with his wife and other advisors, he invented calendars, silkmaking, the 12-tone musical scale, new methods for building bridges and buildings, new forms of medicine, and much more.

唐有虞，号二帝，
相揖逊，称盛世。

Táng yǒu yú, hào èr dì,
xiāng yī xùn, chēng shèng shì.

Tang and Yu, the two emperors,
One abdicated after the other,
theirs was the Age of Prosperity.

唐	táng	Tang
有	yǒu	have
虞	yú	Yu
号	hào	called
二	èr	two
帝	dì	emperor
相	xiāng	one after another
揖	yī	yield
逊	xùn	humble
称	chēng	call
盛	shèng	flourishing
世	shì	age

Tang Yao ruled after the death of the Yellow Emperor. After ruling for seventy years he assembled all the tribal leaders to select his successor. They suggested his son, but Tang replied, "Indeed not! He is devious and quarrelsome. How could he suffice?" They then suggested Yu Shan, a commoner, the son of "an obstinate father and a devious mother" but having filial piety and great intelligence.

Tang tested Yu thoroughly, including marrying him to both of his daughters. Later, Tang gave him the throne. Yu was hardworking and honest. He ruled until age 100, and the people loved him.

夏有禹，商有汤，
周文武，称三王。

Xià yǒu yǔ, shāng yǒu tāng,
zhōu wén wǔ, chēng sān wáng.

The Xia had Yu, the Shang had Tang,
The Zhou had Wen and Wu, these are the Three Kings.

夏	xià	Xia
有	yǒu	have
禹	yǔ	Yu
商	shāng	Shang
有	yǒu	have
汤	tāng	Tang
周	zhōu	Zhou
文	wén	Wen
武	wǔ	Wu
称	chēng	called
三	sān	three
王	wáng	kings

Yu the Great, a descendant of the Yellow Emperor, founded the Xia Dynasty around 2123 BC. He is famed for developing a life-saving flood control system.

Six centuries later the last Xia emperor was overthrown by Cheng Tang in a battle fought during a heavy thunderstorm. Tang, a popular and successful ruler, founded the Shang Dynasty. He ruled for 17 years and greatly expanded his empire.

And six centuries after that, King Wen and his son King Wu led armies that defeated the last Shang king, establishing the Zhou dynasty that ruled for 790 years, the longest in China's history.

夏传子，家天下。
四百载，迁夏社。

Xià chuán zǐ, jiā tiānxià.
Sì bǎi zài, qiān xià shè.

Xia was passed to the child, the hereditary monarchy.
Four hundred years later, the Xia Dynasty ended.

夏	xià	Xia
传	chuán	transmit
子	zǐ	child
家	jiā	family
天	tiān	heaven
下	xià	under
四	sì	four
百	bǎi	hundred
载	zài	years
迁	qiān	change
夏	xià	Xia
社	shè	regime

Yu the Great, Emperor of the Xia Dynasty, ruled for 45 years. He wanted the Minister of Justice to become the next emperor. But the Minister died, so he then selected his friend Boyi who had helped him build his flood control system. But the leaders of the Xia states preferred Yu's son Qi instead, and Yu agreed. Qi ruled for 16 years and was succeeded by his son Tai Kang, followed by 14 more generations.

This tradition of hereditary rule, called jiā tiānxià ("family under heaven") lasted for thousands of years until the Revolution of 1911.

汤伐夏，国号商。
六百载，至纣亡。

Tāng fá xià, guó hào shāng.
Liù bǎi zài, zhì zhòu wáng.

Tang brought down Xia, his dynasty was called Shang.
After six hundred years, it ended with Zhou.

汤	tāng	Tang
伐	fá	cut down
夏	xià	Xia
国	guó	country
号	hào	named
商	shāng	Shang
六	liù	six
百	bǎi	hundred
载	zài	years
至	zhì	until
纣	zhòu	Zhou
亡	wáng	died

Cheng Tang ruled Shang, a small kingdom under the rule of Xia. Under his rule Shang's power grew and gained support from many other Xia kingdoms. The emperor of Xia mistreated his people, soon losing the support of his own generals. So Tang announced that he had to follow the Mandate of Heaven and replace the emperor. He exiled the old emperor, established the Shang Dynasty, and ruled for 17 years. He was a good and wise emperor. He moved the capital to Anyang and built a palace called Xia She in honor of the old Xia dynasty.

周武王，始诛纣。
八百载，最长久。

Zhōu wǔ wáng, shǐ zhū zhòu.
Bā bǎi zài, zuì cháng jiǔ.

King Wu of Zhou executed King Zhou.
Eight hundred years, the longest ever.

周	zhōu	Zhou (Dynasty)
武	wǔ	Wu
王	wáng	king
始	shǐ	in the beginning
诛	zhū	execute
纣	zhòu	Zhou (King)
八	bā	eight
百	bǎi	hundred
载	zài	years
最	zuì	most
长	zhǎng	long
久	jiǔ	time

There are two different Zhou's here! Wu (Ji Fa) was the son of King Wen and the first king of the Zhou (周) Dynasty. His older brother was killed by King Zhou (纣), the king of Shang. So when Wu became king, he worked to destroy the Shang.

In 1046 BC, Wu's 50,000 troops attacked Zhou's capital at the Battle of Muye. Short of soldiers, Zhou armed 170,000 of his slaves but they defected to Wu's side. Zhou fled to his palace, surrounded himself with jewels, and set the palace on fire, dying inside.

周辙东，王纲坠，
逞干戈，尚游说。

Zhōu zhé dōng, wáng gāng zhuì,
chěng gān gē, shàng yóu shuì.

The Zhou made tracks east, loosening the royal bonds,
Showing off shields and spears, listening to traveling sages.

周	zhōu	Zhou
辙	zhé	wagon tracks
东	dōng	east
王	wáng	king
纲	gāng	reign
坠	zhuì	fall apart
逞	chěng	show off
干	gàn	shield
戈	gē	spear
尚	shàng	esteem
游	yóu	travel and persuade
说	shuì	speak

In 770 BC the Zhou Dynasty moved its capital east to Luoyi (present-day Luoyang), starting the Eastern Zhou Dynasty which lasted for 515 years. With less royal control, many small kingdoms within Zhou began declaring their independence, weakening the king and forcing him to rely on them for support. These vassal states banded together under the policy of "Revere the king, expel the barbarians."

Scholars began to travel from one state to another giving advice, ushering in the golden age of Chinese philosophy. Dominating these schools of thought were Confucianism, Legalism and Daoism, but many others also competed for attention.

始春秋，终战国，
五霸强，七雄出。

Shǐ chūn qiū, zhōng zhànguó,
wǔ bà qiáng, qī xióng chū.

Starting with Spring and Autumn,
ending with Warring States,
Five feudal lords ruled, seven kingdoms arose.

始	shǐ	begin
春	chūn	spring
秋	qiū	autumn
终	zhōng	end
战	zhàn	war
国	guó	nation
五	wǔ	five
霸	bà	feudal lord
强	qiáng	master
七	qī	seven
雄	xióng	powerful
出	chū	arise

The beginning of the Eastern Zhou Dynasty, a time of weak central rule, was called the Spring and Autumn period (770-476 BC). The Zhou king had little power, so major decisions were made by a conference of the most powerful princes. The strongest of these were called the Five Hegemons (powerful leaders).

Later came the Warring States period (475–221 BC) when 480 different wars were fought! Finally only the strongest seven states remained: Qin, Han, Wei, Zhao, Qi, Chu and Yan. Then in 221 BC, Qin conquered the rest and formed the Qin Empire, which we now call China.

嬴秦氏，始兼并，
传二世，楚汉争。

Yíng qín shì, shǐ jiān bìng,
chuán èr shì, chǔ hàn zhēng.

The Qin of Ying brought all states together,
Passed to Er Shi, the Chu and Han fought.

嬴	yíng	Ying
秦	qín	Qin
氏	shì	clan
始	shǐ	start
兼	jiān	combine
并	bìng	side by side
传	chuán	pass
二	èr	Er Shi
世	shì	
楚	chǔ	Chu
汉	hàn	Han
争	zhēng	fight

Qin Er Shi's name means "Second generation of Qin." His personal name was Huhai. The youngest of 18 sons, he became the second emperor of Qin but only ruled from 210 to 207 BC. He relied on his powerful prime minister Zhao Gao, who was the real ruler.

Once Zhao presented Er Shi with a deer but called it a horse. The young emperor laughed, saying, "Is the chancellor perhaps mistaken, calling a deer a horse?" Some in the court agreed and called it a deer, others called it a horse. Later, Zhao executed everyone who called it a deer.

高祖兴，汉业建，
至孝平，王莽篡。

Gāozǔ xīng, hàn yè jiàn,
zhì xiào píng, wáng mǎng cuàn.

Gaozu arose, the Han Dynasty was established,
Until Xiao Ping, when Wang Mang seized the throne.

高	gāo	Gaozu
祖	zǔ	
兴	xīng	arose
汉	hàn	Han
业	yè	rule
建	jiàn	establish
至	zhì	until
孝	xiào	Xiao Ping
平	píng	
王	wáng	Wang Mang
莽	mǎng	
篡	cuàn	usurp

The Qin dynasty fell in 206 BC, splintering into 18 small warring kingdoms. Five years later, Gaozu defeated his rivals and took command of the reunified empire, named the Han Dynasty after his home district. Under Gaozu's rule, the Han expelled the Xiongnu (northern nomads) and traded with other nations along the Silk Road.

In 9 AD, Wang Mang seized control from the child emperor Xiao Ping and declared the new Xin Dynasty. But major floods of the Yellow River caused thousands of farmers to lose their lands and rise in rebellion. They stormed the palace and killed Wang Mang.

光武兴，为东汉，
四百年，终於献。

Guāng wǔ xīng, wéi dōng hàn,
sì bǎi nián, zhōng yú xiàn.

Then Guang Wu arose, founding the Eastern Han,
Four hundred years, ended with Xian.

光	guāng	Guang Wu
武	wǔ	
兴	xīng	rise up
为	wéi	called
东	dōng	east
汉	hàn	Han
四	sì	four
百	bǎi	hundred
年	nián	year
终	zhōng	end
於	yú	with
献	xiàn	Xian

In 23 AD, Guang Wu and his allies decisively won the Battle of Kunyang against Wang Mang's 430,000-man Xin Dynasty army. He restored the empire, now called the Eastern Han Dynasty. He ruled for 32 years, eventually controlling nearly all of China. He was a brilliant military strategist, crushing internal rebellions and fighting off incursions from the Mongols and Vietnamese.

The Eastern Han Dynasty lasted 400 years until it became weak from numerous wars and palace intrigues. The last Han ruler, Emperor Xian, gave up the throne in 220 AD, and the empire splintered into three parts.

蜀魏吴，争汉鼎。
号三国，迄两晋。

Shǔ wèi wú, fēn hàn dǐng.
Hào sān guó, qì liǎng jìn.

Shu, Wei and Wu struggled to win Han power.
Called the Three Kingdoms,
it lasted until the Two Jins Dynasty.

蜀	shǔ	Shu
魏	wèi	Wei
吴	wú	Wu
争	fēn	struggle
汉	hàn	Han
鼎	dǐng	trophy => power of the state
号	hào	called
三	sān	three
国	guó	nation
迄	qì	until
两	liǎng	two
晋	jìn	Jin

The three kingdoms of Shu, Wei and Wu battled over the remnants of the Han Dynasty from 220 to 280 AD, leaving a legacy of death and destruction across all of China.

The powerful warlord Cao Cao wrote, "My armor has been worn so long that lice breed in it. Myriad lineages have perished. White bones lie exposed in the fields. For a thousand miles not even a cock is heard. Only one of a hundred survives. Thinking of it rips up my entrails."

With the cities and kingdoms in ruins, it would be three centuries before China was reunited.

宋齐继，梁陈承，
为南朝，都金陵。

Sòng qí jì, liáng chén chéng,
wéi nán cháo, dū jīnlíng.

Then followed the Song and Qi, then the Liang and Chen,
These were the Southern Dynasties, ruled from Jiankang.

宋	sòng	Song
齐	qí	Qi
继	jì	follow after
梁	liáng	Liang
陈	chén	Chen
承	chéng	continue
为	wéi	serve as
南	nán	south
朝	cháo	dynasties
都	dū	capital
金	jīn	Jiankang
陵	líng	

After the Two Jins Dynasty fell in 420 AD, southern China was ruled by four short-lived dynasties: Song for 59 years, Qi for 23 years, Liang for 55 years, and Chen for 12 years. All except Liang had their capital at Jiankang (modern Nanjing). All were led by generals who seized and held power but could not pass power to their heirs.

During this period, intellectuals debated the merits of Daoism, Buddhism and Confucianism. Indian Ocean trade routes grew in importance, making merchants more powerful than aristocrats. But peasants became mercenaries and bandits, and Chen fell to the northern Sui.

71

北元魏，分东西，
宇文周，与高齐。

Běi yuán wèi, fēn dōng xī,
yǔwén zhōu, yǔ gāo qí.

In the north, the Wei of Yuan split into east and west,
Yuwen of Zhou and Gao of Qi.

北	běi	north
元	yuán	Yuan
魏	wèi	Wei
分	fēn	divide
东	dōng	east
西	xī	west
宇	yǔ	Yuwen
文	wén	
周	zhōu	Zhou
与	yǔ	together with
高	gāo	Gao
齐	qí	Qi

Meanwhile, the Northern Wei unified northern China in 439 AD, ending the Sixteen Kingdoms period. Eighty four years later a rebellion of several military garrisons divided the Wei into the Eastern Wei dominated by Han Chinese, and the Western Wei dominated by local tribes. Later, Western Wei became Northern Zhou.

Yuwen Yu, a provincial governor, was invited by the previous emperor's nephew to become emperor. He ruled until a rival poisoned him with sugar cookies. Later, the Northern Qi, led by the Gao family, ruled for 27 years until its defeat by the Northern Zhou.

迨至隋，一土宇，
不再传，失统绪。

Dài zhì suí, yī tǔ yǔ,
bù zài chuán, shī tǒng xù.

*Finally the Sui arrived, uniting under a single house,
not passing it on, it lost the succession.*

迨	dài	until
至	zhì	arrive
隋	suí	Sui
一	yī	one
土	tǔ	earth
宇	yǔ	realm
不	bù	not
再	zài	again
传	chuán	transmit
失	shī	lose
统	tǒng	control
绪	xù	inheritance

After hundreds of years of chaos, the Sui reunited the Northern and Southern dynasties, re-establishing the rule of ethnic Chinese across the entire country. It only lasted 37 years but set the stage for the great Tang Dynasty.

The Sui undertook vast engineering projects including a great canal linking Chang'an (modern Xi'an) to Hangzhou and Beijing, and expanding the Great Wall. Reforms broke up aristocrats' estates and gave farmland to anyone willing to work it. This created abundant food that fueled rapid population growth. But expensive engineering and border wars weakened the government, and rebellion toppled it in 614 AD.

唐高祖，起义师，
除隋乱，创国基。

Táng gāozǔ, qǐyì shī,
chú suí luàn, chuàng guó jī.

Gaozu of Tang led an uprising,
Ended the chaos of Sui, began a new dynasty.

唐	táng	Tang
高	gāo	Gaozu
祖	zǔ	
起	qǐ	raise up
义	yì	righteous
师	shī	army
除	chú	wipe out
隋	suí	Sui
乱	luàn	chaos
创	chuàng	begin
国	guó	nation
基	jī	dynasty

The Tang Dynasty was perhaps the greatest in ancient China. It controlled nearly all of modern-day China except Tibet, and had a population of fifty million. Its capital Chang-an (Xi'an) was the largest city in the world.

Li Yuan (later called Tang Gaozu) was a garrison commander, rose in rebellion and seized the throne to become the first Tang Emperor. Withing ten years he united all of China. He redistributed land to peasants, cut taxes, and reformed the judicial system.

Fearing the rising power of his son Li Shimin, he retired. Shimin replaced him and became the legendary Emperor Taizong.

二十传，三百载，
梁灭之，国乃改。

Èrshí chuán, sān bǎi zǎi,
liáng miè zhī, guó nǎi gǎi.

Twenty transfers in three hundred years,
The Liang destroyed it, the nation was transformed.

二	èr	twenty
十	shí	
传	chuán	transfer
三	sān	three
百	bǎi	hundred
载	zǎi	years
梁	liáng	Liang
灭	miè	extinguish
之	zhī	it
国	guó	country
乃	nǎi	thus
改	gǎi	transform

The Tang Dynasty lasted 289 years. Emperor Taizong's Tang Legal Code listed 500 crimes and prescribed standardized punishments for each, ranging from ten blows with a light stick to execution. A formal civil service examination system assured that the best and brightest were selected for government service. Woodblock printing greatly expanded access to books. Increased trade along the Silk Road and the oceans brought new technologies, new musical instruments, and new thinking in religion and philosophy.

The Tang Dynasty ended when Zhu Wen, a salt smuggler turned military governor turned powerful warlord, killed the emperor and established the Liang Dynasty.

梁唐晋，及汉周，
称五代，皆有由。

Liáng táng jìn, jí hàn zhōu,
chēng wǔ dài, jiē yǒu yóu.

Liang, Tang, Jin, Han and Zhou,
Called the Five Dynasties, each had its reason.

梁	liáng	Liang
唐	táng	Tang
晋	jìn	Jin
及	jí	and
汉	hàn	Han
周	zhōu	Zhou
称	chēng	called
五	wǔ	five
代	dài	dynasties
皆	jiē	each
有	yǒu	has
由	yóu	reason

Zhu Wen named himself Liang Emperor in 907, beginning the first of the Five Dynasties. They were: Later Liang (907-923), Later Tang (923-936), Later Jin (936-946), Later Han (947-950), and Later Zhou (951-960). All five were led by warlords, all were limited to the northern portion of the old Tang Empire, and all ended quickly.

Meanwhile, in the south, the Ten Kingdoms each controlled a region, all more or less at the same time.

Despite the fragmenting of the nation, China experienced cultural and economic growth during this period.

炎宋兴，受周禅，
十八传，南北混。

Yán sòng xìng, shòu zhōu shàn,
shí bā chuán, nán běi hùn.

The fiery Song arose, receiving Zhou's surrender,
Eighteen transfers, south and north fell into chaos.

炎	yán	flame
宋	sòng	Song
兴	xìng	arise
受	shòu	receive
周	zhōu	Zhou
禅	shàn	abdicate
十	shí	eighteen
八	bā	
传	chuán	transfers
南	nán	south
北	běi	north
混	hùn	turmoil

Emperor Taizu led the Song to victory over the Zhou Dynasty in 969, then conquered all Five Dynasties and Ten Kingdoms, reuniting China in 979.

The Song invented a rocket propelled fire arrow shot from gunpowder tubes, and used it to destroy the Southern Tang fleet. The Song also invented gunpowder and developed flamethrowers, explosives, incendiary fire ships and naval artillery. They also invented the compass and were first to issue paper currency. New rice crops brought food surpluses and the population doubled.

There were 18 Song Emperors before the dynasty fell to Kublai Khan's Mongol-led Yuan Dynasty in 1279.

辽与金，帝号纷。
迨灭辽，宋犹存。

Liáo yǔ jīn, dì hào fēn.
Dài miè liáo, sòng yóu cún.

Liao and Jin arose, several emperors were named.
Liao was destroyed, Song remained.

辽	liáo	Liao
与	yǔ	together with
金	jīn	Jin
帝	dì	emperor
号	hào	names
纷	fēn	numerous
迨	dài	annihilate
灭	miè	
辽	liáo	Liao
宋	sòng	Song
犹	yóu	still
存	cún	keep

During the Southern Song Dynasty, the Khitan and Jurchens both claimed to control territory in Northern China. The Khitan called their dynasty the Liao, the Jurchens called theirs the Jin.

In 1115, a tribal chieftan named Aguda united the Khitan tribes and rose up against Liao. Legend says Aguda used a longbow to kill the Liao general in a battle, causing the Liao army to retreat in panic. Aguda then destroyed the Liao and named himself Emperor Taizu of Jin. He allied with the Song Dynasty, forcing the Song to pay annual tribute in silk and silver.

至元兴，金绪歇，
有宋世，一同灭。

Zhì yuán xīng, jīn xù xiē,
Yǒu sòng shì, yītóng miè.

When the Yuan arrived, the Jin line ended,
And the Age of Song was extinguished.

至	zhì	arrive
元	yuán	Yuan
兴	xīng	flourish
金	jīn	Jin
绪	xù	legacy
歇	xiē	end
有	yǒu	have
宋	sòng	Song
世	shì	dynasty
一	yī	together
同	tóng	
灭	miè	extinguish

Genghis Khan united the Mongol tribes and expanded his empire across Asia. His son Ogedei Khan destroyed the Jin Dynasty and conquered most of northern China. Ogedei's son Kublai Khan conquered the Northern and Song Dynasties, placing nearly all of modern day China and Mongolia under his rule.

Kublai's Yuan Dynasty was called the Empire of the Great Khan, the first non-Han dynasty to rule China. A new capital was established in what is now Beijing. Marco Polo served in Kublai's court and wrote that he was a benevolent ruler, building hospitals, reducing taxes, and distributing food to the poor.

并中国，兼戎翟，
明太祖，久亲师。

Bìng zhōngguó, jiān róngdí,
Míng tàizǔ, jiǔ qīn shī.

Uniting China with the barbarian tribes,
Hongwu of Ming led his army in combat.

并	bìng	unite
中	zhōng	middle
国	guó	kingdom
兼	jiān	annex
戎	róng	Rongdi
翟	dí	
明	míng	Ming
太	tài	Taizu
祖	zǔ	
久	jiǔ	long time
亲	qīn	in person
师	shī	army

Zhu Yuanzhang was born a peasant. His family starved in a famine. He became a novice monk, then a wandering beggar. He joined an insurgency at 24 and rose rapidly from footsoldier to commander. His army conquered Nanjing. He was an excellent governor, and the city grew tenfold as people streamed in from the countryside. He directed several successful wars, eventually founding the Ming Dynasty in 1367, becoming Emperor Hongwu (also called Taizu, meaning "the first") and expelling the Mongols from northern China. During his thirty year reign he distributed land to peasant farmers and worked to eliminate government corruption.

传建文，方四祀。
迁北京，永乐嗣。

Chuán jiànwén, fāng sì sì.
Qiān běijīng, yǒnglè sì.

Passed the throne to Jianwen for just four years.
Moved to Beijing, Yongle was his heir.

传	chuán	transfer
建	jiàn	Jianwen
文	wén	
方	fāng	just
四	sì	four
祀	sì	years
迁	qiān	move
北	běi	Beijing
京	jīng	
永	yǒng	Yongle
乐	lè	
嗣	sì	inherit

Zhu Yunwen succeeded his grandfather Emperor Taizu to become the second Ming Emperor. His title, Jianwen Emperor, meant "establish civility" and was a sharp contrast to his grandfather's military conquests. He was a kind ruler, freeing many who had been imprisoned by Emperor Taizu.

He demoted many of his older relatives. In response, his uncle Zhu Di led a rebellion, burning his palace and seizing the throne. Di became the Yongle Emperor and moved the capital to Beijing. Jianwen's body was never found, but many believe he escaped and began a new life as a monk somewhere in Southeast Asia.

逮崇祯，煤山逝。
辽于金，皆称帝。

Dài chóngzhēn, méishān shì.
Liáo yǔ jīn, jiē chēng dì.

Chongzhen came to die on Meishan.
Liao and Jin both called themselves emperor.

逮	dài	arrive
崇	chóng	Chongzhen
祯	zhēn	
煤	méi	Meishan
山	shān	
逝	shì	die
辽	liáo	Liao
于	yǔ	to
金	jīn	Jin
皆	jiē	each
称	chēng	named
帝	dì	emperor

Zhu Youjian, the Chongzhen Emperor, was the 17th and last Ming Dynasty emperor. He succeeded his older brother, taking the throne at age 16.

Centuries of corruption and recent famines had weakened and bankrupted the dynasty. With a major peasant rebellion in the south and a Manchu invasion in the north, his regime could not survive. Rebels attacked the capital in 1644. Chongzhen killed several family members, then walked up Meishan ("coal hill") in a nearby park and hanged himself.

The rebels seized power, but the Manchus rallied support from loyalists and established the new Qing Dynasty a year later.

元灭金，绝宋世。
莅中国，兼戎翟。

Yuán miè jīn, jué sòng shì.
Lì zhōngguó, jiān róngdí.

The Yuan destroyed the Jin, and ended the Song.
They governed China and the barbarian tribes.

元	yuán	Yuan
灭	miè	extinguish
金	jīn	Jin
绝	jué	cut off
宋	sòng	Song
世	shì	dynasty
莅	lì	govern
中	zhōng	China
国	guó	
兼	jiān	annex
戎	róng	barbarians
翟	dí	

In the 1100's the Southern Song ruled southern China and the Jin ruled the north. They fought often, but Song's gunpowder, catapults and bombs allowing them to easily defeat larger Jin forces. Then Genghis Khan's Mongol army invaded and defeated the Jin in 1211.

The Mongols turned their attention to their former allies the Song, attacking from the north, west and south. Kublai Khan blockaded the Yangtze River for five years, finally defeating the Song in 1279 and establishing the Yuan Empire.

Seeing total defeat, Grand Chancellor Lu Xiufu seized the eight year old emperor and leaped into the sea.

九十年，国祚废。

Jiǔ shí nián, guó zuò fèi.

After ninety years, their dynasty ended.

九	jiǔ	ninety
十	shí	
年	nián	year
国	guó	nation
祚	zuò	throne
废	fèi	end

The Yuan Dynasty was part of the Mongol Empire, the greatest empire the world has ever known. It stretched all the way from central Europe in the west to Korea in the east, from Siberia in the north to Vietnam in the south. Their fighting ability was legendary, but they could not maintain rule over such a vast empire.

In China the Mongol-dominated Yuan Dynasty lasted only ninety years, falling to the Ming in 1368.

太祖兴，国大明。
号洪武，都金陵。

Tàizǔ xīng, guó dà míng.
Hào hóngwǔ, dū jīnlíng.

Taizu arose, the Great Ming Dynasty.
His year-title was Hongwu, his capital was Jinling.

太	tài	Taizu
祖	zǔ	
兴	xīng	arose
国	guó	nation
大	dà	Great
明	míng	Ming
号	hào	called
洪	hóng	Hongwu
武	wǔ	
都	dū	capital
金	jīn	Jinling
陵	líng	

The first emperor of any dynasty is called Taizu. This Taizu was named Zhu Yuanzhang. He founded the Ming Dynasty, becoming the Hongwu Emperor, and ruled from 1368 to 1398.

Perhaps his greatest achievement was the Laws of the Great Ming, a code that established harsh but clear laws and closed loopholes used by dishonest officials. Capital punishment was specified for over 1,000 different crimes including embezzlement and chronic idleness. He encouraged agriculture, cut taxes, and moved the capital to Jinling (Nanjing). He also improved the status of slaves, who had been treated as domestic animals under the Tang.

逮成祖，迁燕京。
十七世，至崇祯。

Dài chéngzǔ, qiān yānjīng.
Shí qī shì, zhì chóngzhēn.

Then Chengzu moved the capital to Yanjing.
Seventeen successions, until Chongzhen.

逮	dài	reach
成	chéng	Chengzu
祖	zǔ	
迁	qiān	move
燕	yān	Yanjing
京	jīng	
十	shí	seventeen
七	qī	
世	shì	generations
至	zhì	until
崇	chóng	Chongzhen
祯	zhēn	reach

The Hongwu Emperor's fourth son was Zhu Di (Chengzu). After his father's death, Zhu Di's nephew Zhu Yunwen was named Jianwen Emperor. But the new emperor executed many of his relatives, so Zhu Di rose in rebellion. He overthrew his nephew and was named Yongle Emperor in 1403.

He moved the capital to Yanjing (now Beijing), repaired and reopened the Grand Canal, and directed construction of the Forbidden City and the magnificent Porcelain Tower of Nanjing.

The Ming dynasty lasted until 1644, when the 17th Ming Emperor, Chongzhen, was defeated by a Manchu rebellion that eventually became the Qing Dynasty.

权奄肆，寇如林。
至李闯，神器终。

Quán yān sì, kòu rú lín.
Zhì lǐ chuǎng, shénqì zhōng.

Eunuchs abused their power, bandits as thick as forests.
Li Chuang revolted, burning the ancient artifacts.

权	quán	power
奄	yān	eunuch
肆	sì	tyranny
寇	kòu	bandit
如	rú	like
林	lín	forest
至	zhì	until
李	lǐ	Li Chuang
闯	chuǎng	
神	shén	artifacts
器	qì	
终	zhōng	burn

Li Zicheng (Li Chuang) was born a poor peasant in the decadent Ming Dynasty. He worked as a farmer, blacksmith and mailman. At age 24 he was put in irons for not paying a debt. A group of peasants freed him and named him their leader. Armed with sticks, they ambushed some soldiers and took their weapons. His peasant army grew quickly. His motto was "divide land equally and abolish the grain tax system."

In 1644 his army conquered Beijing and Li was proclaimed Emperor of the new Shun Dynasty. But a month later, Manchu and Ming loyalists defeated him.

清太祖，膺景命。
靖四方，克大定。

Qīng tàizǔ, yīng jǐng mìng.
Jìng sì fāng, kè dà dìng.

The Qing emperor accepted his glorious destiny.
Peace in all directions, victory and stability.

清	qīng	Qing
太	tài	First Emperor
祖	zǔ	
膺	yīng	accept
景	jǐng	glorious
命	mìng	fate
靖	jìng	stabilize
四	sì	four
方	fāng	directions
克	kè	achieve
大	dà	great
定	dìng	stability

The "Qing emperor" was Nurhaci. As a young soldier in Manchuria he fought against and then unified several Jurchen bands. Growing in power, he was attacked by nine other tribes, but his soldiers defeated and reorganized them under the Eight Banners. He then conquered the northeastern province of the Ming Dynasty and proclaimed himself Khan of the Later Jin Dynasty.

Later, his grandson Fulin was named emperor at age 5, with Dorgon "the mastermind of Qing conquest" serving as regent. Fulin took power at age 13 after Dorgon died. Fulin was the first Qing to rule all of China.

廿一史，全在兹。
载治乱，知兴衰。

Niàn yī shǐ, quán zài zī.
Zài zhì luàn, zhī xīng shuāi.

The histories of twenty one dynasties are all here.
They tell of good and bad rule, learn of prosperity and ruin.

廿	niàn	twenty one
一	yī	
史	shǐ	history
全	quán	all
在	zài	exist
兹	zī	herewith
载	zài	record
治	zhì	rule
乱	luàn	chaos
知	zhī	know
兴	xìng	prosperity
衰	shuāi	decline

In ancient China, leadership was non-hereditary and "everything under Heaven belonged to the public" (gōng tiānxià). That changed when Yu the Great founded the first dynasty, the Xia, in 2070 BC and proclaimed that "all under Heaven belongs to the ruling family" (jiā tiānxià).

There have been 70 Chinese dynasties. Some lasted only a month, while the longest, the Shang, lasted for five and a half centuries. The entire Chinese dynastic system lasted for nearly four thousand years until the Revolution of 1911, known as the Xinhai Revolution, overthrew the six-year-old emperor Puyi and brought down Qing, the last dynasty.

Part 4

Confucius saw seven year old Xiang Tuo building sand castles in the road.

- from Part 4, Verse 3

读史者，考实录。
通古今，若亲目。

Dú shǐ zhě, kǎo shílù.
Tōng gǔ jīn, ruò qīn mù.

Read the history books, study the dynastic records.
Connect ancient times to today,
see them with your own eyes.

读	dú	read
史	shǐ	history
者	zhě	books
考	kǎo	examine
实	shí	chronicles
录	lù	
通	tōng	connect
古	gǔ	ancient
今	jīn	today
若	ruò	as
亲	qīn	one's own
目	mù	eye

Truth is more important than life itself.

Cui, a state official, once executed a innocent man accused of a crime. He told his scribe to record the man's death as accidental. The scribe refused so Cui had him killed. The scribe's job was taken by his younger brother. He also refused and Cui had him killed. Same for the third scribe. Finally, the fourth and last brother took the scribe job and also refused to record the lies, saying "you can kill me too, but you cannot change the facts." Cui finally agreed and abandoned his attempts to rewrite history.

口而诵，心而惟。
朝于斯，夕于斯。

Kǒu ér sòng, xīn ér wéi.
Cháo yú sī, xī yú sī.

Speak them with your mouth, ponder them with your heart.
Do it in the morning, do it in the evening.

口	kǒu	mouth
而	ér	cause
诵	sòng	recite
心	xīn	heart
而	ér	cause
惟	wéi	focus
朝	cháo	morning
于	yú	do
斯	sī	this
夕	xī	evening
于	yú	do
斯	sī	this

Learning is the sweet fruit that only grows on bitter roots. You can only master it by studying long and hard.

Fan Zhongyan left his mother and stepfather to live alone. He studied day and night, forgetting to eat and sleep. He kept a pitcher of cold water on his table and poured it on his head whenever he started to fall asleep.

Later he rose to became Prime Minster of the Song Dynasty. He was a famous politician, philosopher, military strategist and poet. He said, "Be the first to bear the world's hardship, the last to enjoy its comfort."

昔仲尼，师项橐。
古圣贤，尚勤学。

Xī zhòng ní, shī xiàng tuó.
Gǔ shèngxián, shàng qín xué.

Once, Zhong Ni had a teacher Xiang Tuo.
The ancient sages were inspired, yet studied diligently.

昔	xī	in the past
仲	zhòng	Zhong Ni
尼	ní	
师	shī	teacher
项	xiàng	Xiang Tuo
橐	tuó	
古	gǔ	ancient
圣	shèng	sage
贤	xián	
尚	shàng	yet
勤	qín	diligent
学	xué	learn

Zhong Ni (Confucius) was riding in a chariot one day with his disciples. He saw seven year old Xiang Tuo building sand castles in the road. Confucius asked him to move aside. The boy refused, saying "whoever heard of moving buildings to make way for carriages?"

Confucius was astounded by this. He wanted to learn more, so he invited him to play a gambling game. Xiang Tuo refused, saying "a gambling king will lose his throne, a gambling farmer will lose his harvest, a gambling student will ignore his studies. I do not gamble."

Xiang Tuo died at age 10.

赵中令，读鲁论。
彼既仕，学且勤。

Zhào zhōnglìng, dú lǔ lùn.
Bǐ jì shì, xué qiě qín.

Grand Secretary Zhao studied the Analects.
Although he was already an official,
he still studied diligently.

赵	zhào	Zhao
中	zhōng	Grand Secretary
令	lìng	
读	dú	read
鲁	lǔ	Lu
论	lùn	Analects
彼	bǐ	that
既	jì	already
仕	shì	official
学	xué	learn
且	qiě	still
勤	qín	diligent

Several versions of the Analects (lúnyǔ) of Confucius have been discovered, including the Lu version mentioned in this verse, the Qi version, and the "old text version" discovered hidden in a wall of Confucius's home.

In the 10th century, Zhao Pu served as Grand Secretary to Emperors Taizu and his younger brother Taizong of the first Song Dynasty. Taizong asked Zhao Pu why he read the Analects, a book commonly taught to children. Zhao replied, "With half of this book I helped your father gain the empire. With the other half I help you preserve it."

披蒲编，削竹简，
彼无书，且知勉。

Pī pú biān, xuē zhú jiǎn,
bǐ wú shū, qiě zhī miǎn.

Splitting and weaving reeds, cutting bamboo slips,
They had no books, but knew how to strive.

披	pī	split
蒲	pú	rush
编	biān	weave
削	xuē	scrape
竹	zhú	bamboo
简	jiǎn	tablet
彼	bǐ	had
无	wú	no
书	shū	book
且	qiě	but
知	zhī	knew
勉	miǎn	endeavor

Learning is hard work, but well worth it.

Lu Wenshu was so poor he could not buy a book, so he cut grasses and wove them together to make books. Later he became a legal specialist, reformer, and astronomer in the Western Han Dynasty.

Gongsun Hong was also born poor, so he cut bamboo slips to learn how to write and learned the Annals at age forty. He began his political career at sixty, and at seventy he became Grand Secretary under the Han Emperor Wu. He stressed the values of sincerity, humaneness, righteousness and moderation, and he loved music.

头悬梁，锥刺股。
彼不教，自勤苦。

Tóu xuán liáng, zhuī cì gǔ.
Bǐ bù jiào, zì qín kǔ.

Tying his hair to a rafter, jabbing his thigh with an awl.
They were not taught, but toiled hard on their own.

头	tóu	head
悬	xuán	suspend
梁	liáng	roof beam
锥	zhuī	awl
刺	cì	stab
股	gǔ	thigh
彼	bǐ	those
不	bù	not
教	jiào	taught
自	zì	self
勤	qín	diligent
苦	kǔ	bitter

Great students do not need others to push them; they push themselves to study and learn. Their hunger for knowledge comes from their hearts.

Sun Jing worked all day and studied all night, he kept himself awake by tying his braided hair to the rafters above so he would be jolted awake if he nodded off. Later he became a famous Confucian scholar.

Su Qin was also very poor, he wanted to study but was very tired. He discovered that he could jab his thigh with a sharp awl to wake himself up. Later he rose to be Prime Minster.

如囊萤，如映雪。
家虽贫，学不辍。

Rú náng yíng, rú yìng xuě.
Jiā suī pín, xué bù chuò.

Putting fireflies in a bag, using the snow's glare.
Though their families were poor, they studied constantly.

如	rú	such as
囊	náng	bag
萤	yíng	firefly
如	rú	such as
映	yìng	reflect
雪	xuě	snow
家	jiā	family
虽	suī	although
贫	pín	poor
学	xué	study
不	bù	not
辍	chuò	cease

Che Yin's family was too poor to afford lamp oil. He desperately wanted to study at night, so he caught fireflies in a bag and hung them up to use as a dim lamp. He became a senior official.

Sun Kang also couldn't afford lamp oil and there were no fireflies in winter, so he went outdoors in the freezing cold and read by moonlight reflected off the snow-covered ground.

Together, these two stories are the root of a Chinese saying, "light from collected fireflies and reflected snow" (náng yíng yìng xuě), referring to anyone who studies hard despite poverty.

如负薪，如挂角。
身虽劳，犹苦卓。

Rú fù xīn, rú guà jiǎo.
Shēn suī láo, yóu kǔ zhuó.

Carrying firewood, herding cattle.
Though they worked hard, they overcame hardships.

如	rú	such as
负	fù	carry
薪	xīn	firewood
如	rú	such as
挂	guà	hang
角	jiǎo	horn
身	shēn	person
虽	suī	despite
劳	láo	toil
犹	yóu	nevertheless
苦	kǔ	bitter
卓	zhuō	outstanding

A Chinese saying "to hang horns from a tree" refers to antelopes that according to legend jump up and hang by their horns from tree branches at night, sleeping safely off the ground. Here, it refers to Li Mi who worked as a cowherd while studying.

Another student, Zhu Maichen, carried firewood for a living, working all day and studying all night. His wife left him. Later he became governor of Guiji. She begged to come back. He poured a bucket of water on the ground and told her, "If you can pick up this spilled water, you may return."

99

苏老泉，二十七，
始发愤，读书籍。

Sū lǎoquán, èrshíqī,
shǐ fā fèn, dú shū jí.

Su Laoquan was twenty seven,
Only then did he show his zeal, studying books and records.

苏	sū	
老	lǎo	Su Laoquan
泉	quán	
二	èr	
十	shí	twenty seven
七	qī	
始	shǐ	only then
发	fā	show
愤	fèn	zeal
读	dú	read
书	shū	book
籍	jí	records

The famous Song Dynasty writer Su Xun, also known as Su Laoquan, did not begin to study seriously until he was 27 years old, which at the time was considered much too old to start learning. Later, he took the civil service examinations but failed them. However, he kept studying hard. Eventually he became a highly respected writer, essayist and the Imperial Librarian.

He had two sons who also became famous writers, Su Shi and Su Zhe. Together, they became known as the "Three Su." Su Xun said he always wished that he had started studying at an earlier age.

彼既老，犹悔迟。
尔小生，宜早思。

Bǐ jì lǎo, yóu huǐ chí.
Ěr xiǎoshēng, yí zǎo sī.

When he was old, he regretted his delay.
And so young ones, think of this early.

彼	bǐ	that
既	jì	already
老	lǎo	old
犹	yóu	still
悔	huǐ	regret
迟	chí	late
尔	ěr	and so
小	xiǎo	young man
生	shēng	
宜	yí	should
早	zǎo	early
思	sī	think

Su Xun's story tells us that when we are young our minds can absorb new information quickly, so youth is the perfect time to begin learning. But it is never too late to start. Even when we are older we should continue to learn.

Su Xun started studying at age 27 and became the Imperial Librarian even though he had no formal education. He also studied history, offering practical solutions to the day's problems based on historical precedents.

Also, there was Gongsun Hong who started learning the Annals of Confucius at age forty and later rose to become Grand Secretary.

若梁灏，八十二，
对大廷，魁多士。

Ruò liáng hào, bāshí'èr,
duì dà tíng, kuí duō shì.

Liang Hao at age eighty two,
His answers in the Great Hall were best of many scholars.

若	ruò	as
梁	liáng	Liang Hao
灏	hào	
八	bā	eighty two
十	shí	
二	èr	
对	duì	reply
大	dà	great
廷	tíng	hall
魁	kuí	chief
多	duō	many
士	shì	scholars

Liang Hao lived during the reign of Song Emperor Zhenzong. Historical records show that he was 23 years old when he became zhuàngyuán, meaning that he placed first in his imperial exams, and he died at age 42.

However, the legend of Liang Hao becoming zhuàngyuán at age 82 has inspired generations of Chinese. Many older people took the exam, often at the same time as their children and grandchildren. Even as late as 1889, eighteen candidates older than age 90 took the imperial exam!

There is a saying in China, "Live to old age by studying to old age."

彼既成，众称异。
尔小生，宜立志。

Bǐ jì chéng, zhòng chēng yì.
Ěr xiǎoshēng, yí lì zhì.

When he succeeded, everyone called him exceptional.
And so, young ones should aim to succeed.

彼	bǐ	he
既	jì	then
成	chéng	succeed
众	zhòng	crowd
称	chēng	praised
异	yì	outstanding
尔	ěr	and so
小	xiǎo	young man
生	shēng	
宜	yí	should
立	lì	aspire
志	zhì	he

For two thousand years, the path to wealth and success in China was to study for and pass the imperial examinations and become appointed to a civil service job. These jobs were awarded based on merit, assuring that the most capable individuals rose to the top. It also ensured that corrupt officials could not build their power base by appointing friends and relatives to positions.

Candidates were locked inside the exam hall for several days and nights, and it was not uncommon for candidates to die from illness or stress. Sometimes only 1% to 2% of candidates passed the exams.

莹八岁，能咏诗。
泌七岁，能赋棋。

Yíng bā suì, néng yǒng shī.
Mì qī suì, néng fù qí.

Ying at eight could write and recite poetry.
Bi at seven could write essays while playing Go.

莹	yíng	Ying
八	bā	eight
岁	suì	years old
能	néng	could
咏	yǒng	chant
诗	shī	poetry
泌	mì	Bi
七	qī	seven
岁	suì	years old
能	néng	could
赋	fù	poetic essay
棋	qí	weiqi ("Go")

Zu Ying lived in the Northern Wei Dynasty. He loved to read, and by age 8 he could compose and sing poetry. His parents worried that he spent too much time studying, so they hid their oil lamp, but late at night he took out the lamps and continue reading.

Once he overslept and hurried to school. It was his turn to recite the from the Book of Documents, but he had left it at home. But he had memorized the book, so he simply recited the entire thing from memory. At age 12 he was appointed a civil servant.

彼颖悟，人称奇，
尔幼学，当效之。

Bǐ yǐng wù, rén chēng qí,
ěr yòu xué, dāng xiào zhī.

They were clever, people called them special,
And so, young students should imitate them.

彼	bǐ	those
颖	yǐng	clever
悟	wù	enlightened
人	rén	people
称	chēng	praised
奇	qí	wonderful
尔	ěr	thus
幼	yòu	young
学	xué	student
当	dāng	should
效	xiào	imitate
之	zhī	them

Li Bi could read and write by age six. Emperor Xuanzong was searching for brilliant young advisors, so he invited the boy to watch the Emperor play the Duke of Yan in a game of wéiqí (Go, a board game similar to chess).

To test the child, the Duke composed a four-line poem (fù) inspired by the game they were playing, then invited Li to do the same. On the spot, Li composed a fù based on the squareness of the board, the roundness of the stones, their movements when they were alive, and their silence when they were dead.

蔡文姬，能辨琴。
谢道韫，能咏吟。

Cài wénjī, néng biàn qín.
Xiè dàoyùn, néng yǒng yín.

Cai Wenji could tell which lute string was broken.
Xie Daoyun could recite poetry.

蔡	cài	
文	wén	Cai Wenji
姬	jī	
能	néng	can
辨	biàn	discriminate
琴	qín	instrument
谢	xiè	
道	dào	Xie Daoyun
韫	yùn	
能	néng	can
咏	yǒng	chant
吟	yín	poetry

Cai Wenji was playing at home while her father played the lute. Suddenly a string broke. Without looking up, she asked, "Father, did the second string break?" He then deliberately broke another string. Again without looking she asked, "And now, did the fourth string break?" She later became a famous poet and musician, but also spent 12 years as the captive wife of Mongol chieftan Liu Bao.

Xie Daoyun was a brilliant child, a skilled debater, a student of literature and philosophy, and an accomplished swordfighter. Her most famous work, "Snow Poem," has been recited for over a thousand years.

彼女子，且聪敏。
尔男子，当自警。

Bǐ nǚzǐ, qiě cōngmǐn.
Ěr nánzǐ, dāng zì jǐng.

They were girls, clever and quick.
You boys should rouse yourselves.

彼	bǐ	those
女	nǚ	girls
子	zi	
且	qiě	and/but
聪	cōng	smart
敏	mǐn	
尔	ěr	you
男	nán	boys
子	zi	
当	dāng	ought
自	zì	oneself
警	jǐng	vigilant

The San Zi Jing was originally written for boys, as were nearly all books and educational materials in ancient China. Families, schools and government were all dominated by men.

Confucius himself said little about the role of women. He considered the dominant role of men to be ordained by heaven, and instructed women to be obedient to their father and older brothers while young, to their husbands while married, and to their sons when widowed.

This all changed after the 1949 revolution, when Mao Zedong said, "Women hold up half the sky" and finally brought Chinese women into equality with men.

107

唐刘晏，方七岁，
举神童，作正字。

Táng liúyàn, fāng qī suì,
jǔ shéntóng, zuò zhèngzì.

Liu Yan of Tang, at age seven,
Was recognized as a child prodigy
and made Corrector of Texts.

唐	táng	Tang
刘	liú	Liu Yan
晏	yàn	
方	fāng	just
七	qī	seven
岁	suì	years old
举	jǔ	recognized as
神	shén	child prodigy
童	tóng	
作	zuò	make
正	zhèng	Corrector of Texts
字	zì	

When Liu Yan was only seven years old, he wrote a song and submitted it to the Tang Emperor Xuanzong. The Emperor was so impressed that he appointed Liu as a scribe in his government, calling him "godly child" (shéntóng). He was made a county magistrate at 17. He continued to serve in a variety of senior government jobs under four different emperors, always capable and always loyal to his country.

When he died at age 65, it was discovered that his family had no real wealth, something almost unheard of for the family of a long-serving and powerful government official.

彼虽幼，身已仕。
尔幼学，勉而致。

Bǐ suī yòu, shēn yǐ shì.
Ěr yòu xué, miǎn ér zhì.

Although a child, he was made an official.
Like this, young ones, you should also exert yourself.

彼	bǐ	he
虽	suī	although
幼	yòu	young
身	shēn	himself
已	yǐ	
仕	shì	official
尔	ěr	like this
幼	yòu	young
学	xué	student
勉	miǎn	make effort
而	ér	also
致	zhì	emulate

Talent is no substitute for hard work. There are many stories of child prodigies in ancient China.

One famous child was Zhongyong, born into a poor farming family. At age 5 he desperately wanted to write and he begged his father for brush, ink and paper. Intrigued, the father agreed, and Zhongyong promptly wrote and signed a poem. His fame spread. Soon he was making money for his family by writing poems. Unfortunately his father didn't bother to give Zhongyong a proper education, and as a teenager his talents disappeared.

Today, "the pity of Zhongyong" is a warning for parents.

有为者，亦若是。

Yǒu wéi zhě, yì ruòshì.

Act like him, succeed like him.

有	yǒu	have
为	wéi	act as
者	zhě	him
亦	yì	also
若	ruò	as if
是	shì	

Confucius believed strongly in the value of hard work. He taught that hard work builds good character, as well as being a strong support for society. In the Analects he says, "Joy can still be found in eating sparingly, drinking plain water and using the upper arm for a pillow. Wealth and status attained immorally are like floating clouds to me."

The Confucian work ethic also includes loyalty to the organization, thrift, dedication, social harmony, a love of education and wisdom, and a concern for social propriety.

This belief has contributed to China's prosperity, much like Protestantism in Western countries.

The old woman replied, "I will grind this pestle into a needle, no matter how thick and hard it is."

- from Part 5, Verse 6

犬守夜，鸡司晨。
苟不学，曷为人？

Quǎn shǒu yè, jī sī chén.
Gǒu bù xué, hé wéi rén?

The dog guards the night, the rooster proclaims the dawn.
If you fail to learn, how can you become a person?

犬	quǎn	dog
守	shǒu	guard
夜	yè	night
鸡	jī	chicken
司	sī	take charge of
晨	chén	morning
苟	gǒu	if
不	bù	not
学	xué	learn
曷	hé	how
为	wèi	to be
人	rén	person

How are people different from animals? The dog and the rooster work hard at their jobs, but they are born already knowing how to do those jobs. The dog guards and the rooster crows by instinct. But people must also learn how to be human, how to live in the world, and how to be productive members of their society. Animals can sometimes adapt to the world around them, but only humans can learn how to change the world, hopefully for the better.

Confucius tells us to work hard to become a learned person (jūnzì) and eventually a sage (shèngxián).

蚕吐丝，蜂酿蜜。
人不学，不如物。

Cán tǔ sī, fēng niàng mì.
Rén bù xué, bùrú wù.

The silkworm spins silk, the bee makes honey.
If a person does not learn, isn't he like an animal?

蚕	cán	silkworm
吐	tǔ	spits
丝	sī	silk
蜂	fēng	bee
酿	niàng	brews
蜜	mì	honey
人	rén	people
不	bù	not
学	xué	learn
不	bù	not
如	rú	as
物	wù	creature

Silkworms and bees are perhaps the most hardworking in the animal kingdom, spending their lives in selfless dedication to their tasks. This is to be admired, but people need to do more than work, and we need to learn more than our jobs. We need to learn the right way to live in society.

Zengzi, a disciple of Confucius, said that the way of Confucianism is just two things. First is loyalty (zhōng), being true in all relationships, including those above and below you. Second is self-reflection (shù): "what you do not desire for yourself, do not do to others."

113

幼而学，壮而行。
上致君，下泽民。

Yòu ér xué, zhuàng ér xíng.
Shàng zhì jūn, xià zé mín.

Learn when you are young, act when you are grown.
Support the ruler above, benefit the people below.

幼	yòu	young
而	ér	then
学	xué	learn
壮	zhuàng	sturdy
而	ér	then
行	xíng	do what is learned
上	shàng	above
致	zhì	help to achieve
君	jūn	ruler
下	xià	below
泽	zé	fertilize
民	mín	people

Confucius taught that there are five relationships that create a harmonious society, like a great wheel turning on a strong axis. Ruler to subject (jūnchén): a ruler of a nation should be like a father, ruling through example instead of power. Father to son (fùzǐ): filial piety, the most important, because the role of a parent when rooted in love and compassion can be applied to many different situations. Husband to wife (fūfù): based on love, compassion and respect. Older brother to younger brother (xiōngdì): passing down teachings of right and wrong. Between friends (péngyǒu): mutual trust and respect.

扬名声，显父母。
光于前，裕于后。

Yángmíng shēng, xiǎn fùmǔ.
Guāng yú qián, yù yú hòu.

Make a name for yourself, glorify your parents.
Shine light on your ancestors,
prosperity to your descendants.

扬	yáng	fame
名	míng	
声	shēng	sound
显	xiǎn	illuminate
父	fù	father
母	mǔ	mother
光	guāng	bright
于	yú	on
前	qián	before
裕	yù	abundant
于	yú	on
后	hòu	after

Confucius strongly believed that rituals and ceremonies could unite people and strengthen community. One of the most important rituals was reverence (jìng) for one's ancestors.

Confucius said, "Observe what a person plans to do when his father is alive, and then observe what he actually does when his father is dead. If for three years he makes no changes to his father's ways, he can be said to be a good son."

The ancient Chinese believed that if peope don't show reverence for ancestors, their ghosts could rise from their graves and wander the earth, causing trouble for the living.

人遗子，金满籯。
我教子，惟一经。

Rén yí zi, jīn mǎn yíng.
Wǒ jiàozǐ, wéiyī jīng.

Others leave their children chests full of gold.
I teach children just this one classic.

人	rén	others
遗	yí	leave behind
子	zi	child
金	jīn	gold
满	mǎn	full
籯	yíng	basket
我	wǒ	I
教	jiào	teach
子	zi	child
惟	wéi	only
一	yī	one
经	jīng	classic

There's a saying, "wealth doesn't last three generations." The first generation works hard to create wealth, the second can only preserve it, and the third loses it all. So instead of giving your children gold, teach them Confucius's principles of moral living.

This book gives you a summary of those principles. Remember: the father is loving, the son is filial. The elder brother is caring, the younger brother is respectful. The husband behaves righteously, the wife is willing to follow him. The ruler cares for his subjects, the officials are loyal to him. And everyone treats their friends like family.

勤有功，戏无益。
戒之哉，宜勉力。

Qín yǒu gōng, xì wú yì.
Jiè zhī zāi, yí miǎn lì.

Hard work has value, play gives no advantage.
Stay vigilant, do your best.

勤	qín	diligence
有	yǒu	has
功	gōng	merit
戏	xì	play
无	wú	no
益	yì	advantage
戒	jiè	guard
之	zhī	it
哉	zāi	ah!
宜	yí	should
勉	miǎn	do your best
力	lì	diligence

As a boy Li Bai never studied, he would rather play outside. One day he saw an old woman sitting on a riverbank, grinding grain with an iron pestle. "People who do this are fools!" he cried. She replied, "I will grind this pestle into a needle, no matter how thick and hard it is." Li Bai tried it but gave up after a minute. But he kept thinking about the woman, her words, and her work. Gradually he became a good student, and eventually a famous poet.

Remember, great knowledge always requires grinding an iron pestle into a needle.

RESOURCES FOR LEARNING

Want to learn more about the verses you've just read? For each verse, we've collected a variety of different sources of information to give you lots of different points of view. If you want to see that web page to read the article, the easiest way is to use a smartphone to take a picture of the QR code that's in the lower right corner of the page.   That will take you directly to the web page.

Of course, you can also just type in the web address in the list below.

Note that we don't control these websites, and it's always possible that some of the websites may be unavailable. We apologize in advance if this happens to you!

Part 1

Verse	Learn More
1	Hays, Jeffrey. "Children and Child Rearing Customs in China." *Facts and Details,* factsanddetails.com. 2008-2015. http://factsanddetails.com/china/cat4/sub21/item103.html
2	"Zhou Chu who eliminated the three calamities." In UsingEnglish.com. "The Three Character Classic (San Zi Jing)" 8-May-2016. https://www.usingenglish.com/forum/threads/238401-Zhou-Chu-who-eliminated-the-three-calamities-(A-story-from-ancient-China-)
3	"Famous People From Ancient China: Mencius and His Mother", *Vision Times*, 24-Jun-2017. https://www.visiontimes.com/2017/06/24/stories-of-famous-people-from-ancient-china-menciuss-mother.html
4	Humble, Geoff. "Secret Virtue of the Dou Lineage." *Zhiguai Translations - Chinese Tales of the Strange and Anomalous,* Geoff Humble, 04-May-2018. https://huhaixinwen.wordpress.com/2018/05/04/secret-virtue-of-the-dou-lineage-竇氏陰德/

5	"Zeng Guofan (Tseng Kuo-fan)." *Age of Revolution: Revolutions and empires in the world history*, Oct-2010. http://historyworldsome.blogspot.com/2013/10/zeng-guofan-tseng-kuo-fan.html
6	Khurana, Simran. "47 Confucius Quotes That Still Ring True Today." *ThoughtCo,* Dotdash Press, 03-Jul-2019. https://www.thoughtco.com/best-confucius-quotes-2833291
7	"Celebrating the Confucian Work Ethic." *The Confucian Weekly Bulletin,* Centre for East-West Cultural and Economic Studies, 20-May-2015. https://confucianweeklybulletin.wordpress.com/2015/05/01/celebrating-the-confucian-work-ethic/
8	Chen, Judy. "Stand In the Snow Waiting For Master Cheng." Medium, 18-July-2015. https://medium.com/@zhang782/stand-in-the-snow-waiting-for-master-cheng-4402dc1043fa
9	Gou Shouzheng. "The Twenty-Four Paragons of Filial Piety. Number Nineteen: He Fanned the Pillows and Warmed the Sheets: Huang Xiang." http://www.ruf.rice.edu/~asia/24ParagonsFilialPiety.html
10	"Kong Rong Gave Away Bigger Pears." eChineseLearning, 12-Aug-2015. https://www.echineselearning.com/blog/kong-rong-rang-li-kong-rong-gave-away-bigger-pears-2
11	Teon, Aris, "Filial Piety (孝) in Chinese Culture." *The Greater China Journal*, Automattic Inc., 14-Mar-2016. https://china-journal.org/2016/03/14/filial-piety-in-chinese-culture/
12	Kelsey, Suzie. "Everything You Need to Know about Chinese Numbers", *Closemaster Blog*, Language Innovation LLC, 29-Dec-2019. https://www.clozemaster.com/blog/chinese-numbers/
13	"Story of Wan Hu – The first astronaut in the world", *Paviavio*, 8-Oct-2009. https://paviavio.wordpress.com/2009/10/08/story-of-wan-hu-the-first-astronaut-in-the-world/
14	"Chinese medicine during the Qin and Han dynasties (221 BCE - 220 CE)." *The Holosapiens Project.* https://holosapiens.com/history/chinese-medicine-during-the-qin-and-han-dynasties-221-bce-581-ce

15	"The Candle Dragon", *Chinese Moment blog*, 20-Nov-2019. https://www.chinesemoment.com/chinese-culture/the-candle-dragon-zhu-long-2/
16	Zhang Qian, "Yellow Emperor Victorious in Zhuolu Battle", *Shanghai Daily*, 13-Oct-2018. https://archive.shine.cn/feature/art-and-culture/Yellow-Emperor-victorious-in-Zhuolu-Battle/shdaily.shtml
17	"Yu the Great", *Travel China Guide*, 6-Nov-2018. https://www.travelchinaguide.com/intro/history/prehistoric/great_yu.htm
18	"Philosophy 312: Oriental Philosophy, Main Concepts of Confucianism", Lander University. https://philosophy.lander.edu/oriental/main.html
19	Adhikari, Saugat. "Top 10 Traditional Ancient Chinese Foods." *Ancient History Lists*, 4-Jun-2019. https://www.ancienthistorylists.com/china-history/top-10-traditional-ancient-chinese-foods/
20	Mark, Joshua. "Dogs in Ancient China." *Ancient History Encyclopedia*, Ancient History Encyclopedia Foundation, 31-Jan-2019. https://www.ancient.eu/article/1327/dogs-in-ancient-china/
21	"Du Zichun." *Chinese Mythology Podcast.* 9-Sep-2019. https://chinesemythologypodcast.com/2019/09/09/episode-185-du-zichun-part-1/
22	Bennet, James. "Get to Know These 7 Traditional Chinese Instruments." *New York Public Radio*. https://www.wqxr.org/story/get-know-these-7-traditional-chinese-instruments/
23	Mack, Lauren. "Filial Piety: An Important Chinese Cultural Value." *ThoughtCo*, Feb. 11, 2020. www.thoughtco.com/filial-piety-in-chinese-688386
24	Cui Hui'ao, You Siyuan. "Filial piety still valued in contemporary China." *CGTN Live*, CGTN, 3-Jul-2018. https://news.cgtn.com/news/3d3d514e3151544e78457a6333566d54/share_p.html

25	Brians, Paul et al. "Examples of Filial Piety (14th Century CE)." From Reading About the World. https://www2.kenyon.edu/Depts/Religion/Fac/Adler/Reln270/24-filial1.htm
26	Belludi, Nagesh. "Confucius on Dealing with People." *Right Attitudes*, Genesis Framework, 29-Jul-2016. https://www.rightattitudes.com/2016/07/29/confucius-on-dealing-with-people/
27	Kuek, Kerby. "Kids must learn reality bites". The Standard. 14-Mar-2017. https://www.thestandard.com.hk/sections-news-print/180723/Kids-must-learn-reality-bites

Part 2

Verse	Learn More
1	"Ancient China Writing." *Coolaboo*. https://www.coolaboo.com/world-history/ancient-china/ancient-china-writing/
2	"Four Books and Five Classics of the Ancient China." *Short History Website*. 14-Jun-2016. https://www.shorthistory.org/ancient-civilizations/ancient-china/the-five-classics-of-the-ancient-china/
3	Davis, M. H. and Chow-Leung. "A Story from Confucius." *Chinese Fables and Folk Stories*, Kessinger Publishing, 2008. https://americanliterature.com/author/confucius/short-story/a-story-from-confucius
4	Stefon, Matt, et al. "Mencius, Chinese Philosopher." *Encyclopedia Brittanica*. https://www.britannica.com/biography/Mencius-Chinese-philosopher
5	"Confucius, Mencius and Zisi can still teach us about a healthy lifestyle." *The Confucian Weekly Bulletin*, Bond University's Centre for East-West Cultural and Economic Studies, 11-Mar-2016. https://confucianweeklybulletin.wordpress.com/2016/03/11/confucius-mencius-and-zisi-can-still-teach-us-about-a-healthy-lifestyle-by-alessandro-benedetti-content-writer/
6	"The Great Learning - Authorship and Context," Student Guide to World Philosophy Ed. John K. Roth, Christina J. Moose and Rowena Wildin. *eNotes.com*, 9-Jun-2020. https://www.enotes.com/topics/great-learning/biography#biography-authorship-and-context

7	Sun Jiahui, "Bizarre Tales of Filial Piety." *The World of Chinese*, The Commercial Press, 29-Jan-2015. https://www.theworldofchinese.com/2015/01/bizarre-tales-of-filial-piety/
8	Theobald, Ulrich. "jing 經, the Confucian Classics." *ChinaKnowledge.de*, Ulrich Theobald, 10-Jun-2010. http://www.chinaknowledge.de/Literature/Terms/classics.html
9	Weinberger, Eliot. "What is the I Ching?", *ChinaFile*, Asia Society, 25-Feb-2016. https://www.chinafile.com/library/nyrb-china-archive/what-i-ching
10	Theobald, Ulrich. "Shangshu or Shujing." *ChinaKnowledge.de*, Ulrich Theobald, 24-Jul-2010. http://www.chinaknowledge.de/Literature/Classics/shangshu.html
11	"Duke of Zhou: Paragon of Confucian Virtue." *Facts and Details*, factsanddetails.com, Sep-2016. http://factsanddetails.com/china/cat2/sub2/entry-5404.html
12	Wang, Ralph. "Great Unity." *KidSpirit*, KidSpirit Inc., 12-Sep-2017. https://kidspiritonline.com/magazine/unity-and-division/great-unity/
13	Jordan, David K. "Blue-Collared Lad (Four Ancient Chinese Songs)." *David K. Jordan's personal pages*, University of California San Diego, 14-Nov-2013. https://pages.ucsd.edu/~dkjordan/chin/chtxts/ShyJing.html
14	Jordan, David K. "The Spring & Autumn Annals and the Zuǒ Zhuàn." *David K. Jordan's personal pages*, University of California San Diego. https://pages.ucsd.edu/~dkjordan/chin/Koong/TzuooJuanne.html
15	Liu, Stephen. "Zheng Bo defeated Duan in Yan." *StphnLiu 的博客 Blog*, SINA Corporation, 20-May-2011. http://blog.sina.com.cn/s/blog_4fc736710100qyen.html
16	"Two Stories of Confucius: An Eye into China's Principle of "Non-interference in Internal Affairs", *The Daily Trust*, Embassy of the People's Republic of China in the Federal Republic of Nigeria, 02-Aug-2012. http://ng.china-embassy.org/eng/xw/t957799.htm

17	"Ethnicity, Orthodoxy, and Policy in Medieval China: The Political Philosophy of Wang Tong (584?-617)." Leiden University. https://www.universiteitleiden.nl/en/research/research-projects/humanities/ethnicity-orthodoxy-and-policy-in-medieval-china-the-political-philosophy-of-wang-tong-584-617

Part 3

Verse	Learn More
1	Donn, Lin. "China's Dynastic Cycle." *Ancient China for Kids*, Lin & Don Donn. https://china.mrdonn.org/dynastic-cycle.html
2	Donn, Lin. "The Silk Road." *Ancient China for Kids*, Lin & Don Donn. https://china.mrdonn.org/silk.html
3	Hays, Jeffrey. "Three Great Sage Kings: Emperors Yao, Shun and Yu." *Facts and Details*, factsanddetails.com, Nov-2009. http://factsanddetails.com/china/cat2/sub1/entry-5387.html
4	"Zhou Dynasty (1046 – 256 BC)." *Chinese History Digest*, 2014. http://www.chinesehistorydigest.com/zhoudynasty.html
5	"Xia Dynasty Facts." *SoftSchools.com*. https://www.softschools.com/facts/ancient_civilizations/xia_dynasty_facts/3238/
6	Mark, Emily. "Shang Dynasty," *Ancient History Encyclopedia*, www.ancient.eu.com, 28-Jan-2016. https://www.ancient.eu/Shang_Dynasty/
7	Abbe, Olivia. "Historic Battles Series: Battle of Muye – 1046 BCE." *NYK Daily*, nykdaily, 9-May-2020. https://nykdaily.com/2020/05/historic-battles-series-battle-of-muye-1046-bce/
8	Quesada, Michael. "The 100 Schools Of Thought In Ancient China." *Kaiya*, Asian Art, 11-Jul-2018. https://kaiya.co/blogs/news/the-100-schools-of-thought-in-ancient-china

9	Watkins, Thayer. "The Warring States Period of Ancient China, 480 BCE to 221 BCE." *San Jose State University Department of Economics.* https://www.sjsu.edu/faculty/watkins/warringstates.htm
10	Bitfish. "Calling a deer a horse — Chinese Idiom." *Your Chinese Story*, A Medium Corporation, 29-Jul-2019. https://medium.com/your-chinese-story/calling-a-deer-a-horse-chinese-idiom-8bf62cc1ff10
11	Smitha, Frank E. "Failed Reform and Chaos." *Dynastic Rule and the Chinese*, Frank E. Smitha. http://www.fsmitha.com/h1/china05.htm
12	"Emperor Guangwu of Han China." *Academic Kids Encyclopedia*, 7-Mar-2005. https://academickids.com/encyclopedia/index.php/Emperor_Guangwu_of_Han_China
13	Cartwright, Mark. "The Early Three Kingdoms Period." *Ancient History Encyclopedia*, www.ancient.eu.com, 12-Jan-2018. https://www.ancient.eu/article/1174/the-early-three-kingdoms-period/
14	"Southern Dynasties." *China & Asia Cultural Travel*, Tansuo CulturalTravel Solution Ltd. https://www.asiaculturaltravel.co.uk/southern-dynasties/
15	"Northern and Southern Dynasties." *Wikipedia*, The Wikimedia Foundation. https://en.wikipedia.org/wiki/Northern_and_Southern_dynasties#Southern_dynasties
16	"China's Grand Canal or Emperor's Canal." *Chinasage*, Chinasage, 2-Dec-2016. http://www.chinasage.info/grand-canal.htm
17	"Tang Gaozu." *ChinaCulture.org*, Feb-2008. http://en.chinaculture.org/library/2008-02/09/content_22869.htm
18	Teon, Aris. "China's Legal System and the Ten Abominations." *The Greater China Journal,* Automattic, 11-May-2016. https://china-journal.org/2016/05/11/china-legal-system-ten-abominations/
19	"Five Dynasties of China." *Epic World History*, 2013. http://epicworldhistory.blogspot.com/2013/10/five-dynasties-of-china.html

20	Ebrey, Patricia. "Gunpowder and Firearms." *A Visual Sourcebook of Chinese Civilization*, University of Washington. https://depts.washington.edu/chinaciv/miltech/firearms.htm
21	"Song, Liao, Jin, and Western Xia dynasties." *FollowCN.com*, 14-Jan-2017. https://history.followcn.com/2017/01/14/song-liao-jin-and-western-xia-dynasties/
22	Johnson, Jean. "The Mongol Dynasty; When Kublai Khan Ruled China." *Asia Society's Center for Global Education*, Asia Society. https://asiasociety.org/education/mongol-dynasty
23	"Zhu Yuanzhang — A Beggar, Monk, Soldier, and Founder Emperor of the Ming Dynasty." *China Culture*, ChinaFetching. https://www.chinafetching.com/zhu-yuanzhang
24	"Ming Emperor overseas?" *Chinatownology*, Chinatownology, 2007-2015. http://www.chinatownology.com/ming_emperor_overseas.html
25	Cock-Starkey, Claire. "Ahi Haui – The 'Guilty' Pagoda Tree." *Nonfictioness*, 19-Oct-2017. https://nonfictioness.com/2017/10/19/zui-haui-the-guilty-pagoda-tree/
26	Jenne, Jeremiah. "The End of the Song." *Here Dongguan Magazine*, 15-Dec-2015. https://www.heredg.com/2015/12/the-end-of-the-song/
27	Cartwright, Mark. "Mongol Empire." *Ancient History Encyclopedia*, Ancient History Encyclopedia Foundation, 11-Nov-2019. https://www.ancient.eu/Mongol_Empire/
28	"The Great Qing Code: Law and Order During China's Last Dynasty." *Constitutional Rights Foundation*, 2015. https://www.crf-usa.org/images/pdf/gates/The-great-qing-code.pdf
29	Szczepanski, Kallie. "Biography of Zhu Di, China's Yongle Emperor", *ThoughtCo,* Dotdash Press, 3-Jul-2019. https://www.thoughtco.com/the-yongle-emperor-zhu-di-195231
30	Hua Yu, Ma Quan. "马泉 (Maoist era propaganda posters glorifying Li Zicheng)." *International Institute of Social History*, Royal Netherlands Academy of Arts and Sciences, 1982. https://hdl.handle.net/10622/E4B2688F-D47B-4A7D-91C4-

	ED5E7D24EC93
31	"Nurhachi and the system of 'Eight Banner'." *Science Museums of China*, Chinese Academy of Sciences. http://www.kepu.net.cn/english/nationalityne/man/200312050050.html
32	Tsin, Michael. "The Dynasties Song", in "Timeline of Chinese History and Dynasties", *Asia for Educators*, Columbia University, 1995. http://afe.easia.columbia.edu/timelines/china_timeline.htm#song

Part 4

Verse	Learn More
1	"China: Traditions and Transformations Open Learning Course" (course available for free, requires registration), *Harvard Extension School*. https://www.extension.harvard.edu/open-learning-initiative/china-history
2	"Fan Zhongyan - Poems & Ci-Lyrics of the Song Dynasty". *Baby Growths*, retrieved from the Wayback Machine. https://web.archive.org/web/20120323100905/http://www.baby-growths.com/fan-zhongyan-poems-ci-song-dynasty/
3	Lok, David. "Confucius and Xiang Tuo." *The Banknote Den,* David Lok. http://www.banknoteden.com/TMFOM/China.html
4	"Analects Study Guide." *Course Hero*. 5-Oct-2017. https://www.coursehero.com/lit/Analects/
5	Song, Yirui. "The Studious Spirit of the Chinese." *The Splended Chinese Culture*, The Academy of Chinese Studies, 2015. https://en.chiculture.net/?file=topic_details&old_id=0306
6	Sun Jiahui. "Hard workers of an ancient era." *The World of Chinese Magazine,* 23-Apr-2015. https://www.theworldofchinese.com/2015/04/hard-workers-of-an-ancient-era/

7	Wang, Betty. "A+ With the Ancients." *Shen Yun Performing Arts Blog*, Shen Yun Performing Arts 22-Oct-2015. https://www.shenyunperformingarts.org/blog/view/article/e/XdtJHdW2Sr4/study-tips-learn-from-the-ancients
8	Oestreich, James R. "Revenge in a Bowl, Served Cold." *The New York Times*, 22-May-2012. https://www.nytimes.com/2012/05/23/arts/music/shanghai-troupe-presents-ancient-opera-at-asia-society.html
9	"The Three Su: a Father and Two Sons-Sequel 1." *Chinesegeography blog*, 6-Apr-2013. https://chinesegeography.skyrock.com/3154318192-The-Three-Su-a-Father-and-Two-Sons-Sequel.html
10	Peng Quingsheng. "Eight Great Prose Masters of Tang and Song." *Splendid Chi Culture*, The Academy of Chinese Studies Ltd., 14-Aug-2019. https://chiculture.org.hk/en/china-five-thousand-years/1940
11	"2,000 years of Examinations in China." *Chinasage*, 2016. http://www.chinasage.info/examinations.htm
12	Jiao, Bunny. "Sit For the Exam, Fight For the Rank." *The World of Chinese Magazine*,, 6-Jun-2013. https://www.theworldofchinese.com/2013/06/sit-for-the-exam-fight-for-the-rank/
13	Giles, Herbert. *San Tzu Ching Translated and Annotated*. Kelly & Watson, 1900, in *Wikisource*. https://en.wikisource.org/wiki/Page:Elementary_Chinese_-_San_Tzu_Ching_(1900).djvu/152
14	Xu Lei. "Chapter Five of the Great Tang Surprise, Focusing on Lingwu." *iShare Chinese Culture*. https://culture.ilove-map.com/en/novel/detail/5d85cdf044e69c194c649f19.html
15	"Xie Daoyun." *FollowCN Chinese Women*, Followcn, 15-Jun-2018. https://www.followcn.com/women/2018/06/15/xie-daoyun/
16	"Traditional Women's Roles in China." *Facts and Details*, factsanddetails.com, 2019. http://factsanddetails.com/china/cat3/sub9/entry-5562.html#chapter-3

Verse	Learn More
17	Pearce, Jade. "The Thrifty Prime Minister" in "Dizi Gui (弟子规) : Valuing Character Over Affluence)." *The Epoch Times Singapore Edition*, The Epoch Times Pte Ltd., 5-Mar-2019. https://epochtimes.today/valuing-character-over-affluence/
18	Sun Jiahui, "Child Prodigies of Ancient Eras." *The World of Chinese Magazine,* (2015). https://www.theworldofchinese.com/2015/02/child-prodigies-of-ancient-eras/
19	"Celebrating the Confucian Work Ethic." *The Confucian Weekly Bulletin*, 1-May-2015. https://confucianweeklybulletin.wordpress.com/2015/05/01/celebrating-the-confucian-work-ethic/

Part 5

Verse	Learn More
1	Lafleur, Robert. "The Pedagogy of Confucius." *The Great Courses Daily*, The Teaching Company Sales, LLC, 5-Jul-2017. https://www.thegreatcoursesdaily.com/the-pedagogy-of-confucius/
2	Richey, Jeffrey. "Principles of Moral Thought and Action." *Patheos Religion Library: Confucianism*, Patheos. https://www.patheos.com/library/confucianism/ethics-morality-community/principles-of-moral-thought-and-action
3	Hellums, Frances. "Confucius Five Relationships." *St. John's School Wiki*, St. John's School, 24-Apr-2013. http://wiki.sjs.org/wiki/index.php/Confucius_Five_relationships
4	Richey, Jeffrey. "Rites and Ceremonies." *Patheos Religion Library: Confucianism*, Patheos. https://www.patheos.com/library/confucianism/ritual-worship-devotion-symbolism/rites-and-ceremonies
5	Liew, Cindy. "Tips From Confucius on Living a Harmonious Family Life." *The Epoch Times Singapore Edition*, The Epoch Times Pte Ltd, 5-Oct-2018. https://epochtimes.today/confucius-living-a-harmonious-family-life-the-confucian-way/
6	"Grinding an Iron Pestle into a Needle." *eChineseLearning*, eChineseLearning.com, 15-Dec-2009. https://www.echineselearning.com/blog/mochuchengzhen-grinding-an-iron-pestle-into-a-needle

RESOURCES FOR RESEARCH

If you enjoyed this book, you might really enjoy going online and digging into the source materials yourself. The San Zi Jing is over 800 years old and the original Chinese sources are extremely difficult to read, but there are some great online research resources. To access these online resources, take a picture of the QR codes below with a smartphone and follow the link, or of course you can just type in the web address.

To start your research, your first stop should be two classic English-language translations written by British scholars. The first was by E.J. Eitel in 1892. It was followed in 1900 by a much better translation by Herbert Giles which is still considered the standard translation today. Fortunately, both are available for free online:

Eitel, E.J., "Chinese School-Books, The Tri-Metrical Classic." *The China Review, Or, Notes and Queries on the Far East, Volume 20, 1892-1893*, pages 35-41. Kelly & Walsh, Shanghai (1893).

https://books.google.com/books?id=oR5BAQAA
MAAJ&pg=PA40&lpg=PA40&dq=lu+wenshu+sch
olar&source=bl&ots=B_ueK_Q0UD&sig=ACfU3U
0ODGwRCPL59VhhatWsnQ9TZRDIcQ&hl=en&sa
=X&ved=2ahUKEwjvq5G5_8_pAhX6lXIEHXcEBnw
Q6AEwCHoECAoQAQ#v=onepage&q=%E8%8B%
8F%E8%80%81%E6%B3%89&f=false

Wang, Yinglin; Giles, Herbert Allen,. "San Tzu Ching Translated and Annotated." Kelly & Watson, 1900. https://archive.org/stream/elementarychines00wangrich

An excellent 2007 bibliography of San Zi Jing translations, many available online, is here:

Shea, Marilyn, "Bibliography for the San Zi Jing and Related Chinese Texts." University of Maine at Farmington, 2007. http://hua.umf.maine.edu/Chinese/stories/sanzijing/sanzijingbiblio.html

If you want to dive deeper into the meaning of each word, there are websites that let you step through the book verse-by-verse and character-by-character, displaying the meanings of each word so you can create your own translation (though beware, the definitions of some archaic words are inaccurate). The best websites we've found for this are:

"三字經 - Three Character Classic." *Chinese Text Project.* https://ctext.org/three-character-classic , click the blue double-arrow icons to explore each verse.

"三字經 [Sanzi Jing] Three-Character Classic: A Confucian Roadmap for Kids." *Yellowbridge.* https://www.yellowbridge.com/onlinelit/sanzijing.php

Several Chinese language websites provide the San Zi Jing along with translation and commentary. If you use a web browser with a translation feature, such as Chrome, you can let the browser automatically translate the page, although the resulting translation is usually pretty poor. Our favorites are:

"San Zi Jing." *Guoxuemeng.*
http://www.guoxuemeng.com/guoxue/sanzijing

"San Zi Jing." Sinology. http://3.5000yan.com/

And finally, if you really want to take a deep dive into the deeper meaning and histories of obscure Chinese character, visit:

Baidu. https://baike.baidu.com/

Just enter the Chinese character you're interested in into the search bar. Again, make sure you use the translation feature of your web browser.

ABOUT THE AUTHORS

Wang Yinglin (王應麟) (1223-1296) was a philosopher, historian, astronomer and writer in the late Southern Song Dynasty. It is said that he spent 14 years preparing to take the imperial examination, which he passed at age 32. He was a Confucian scholar who stressed the importance of applying the teachings of the Confucian Classics to practical governance. He authored many books including the 100-chapter *Jade Sea Encyclopedia*. He is also believed to have written the first version of the *San Zi Jing*, though this has never been confirmed.

Jeff Pepper has worked for thirty years in the computer software business, where he has started and led several successful tech companies, authored two software related books, and was awarded three U.S. software patents. In 2017 he started Imagin8 Press (www.imagin8press.com) to serve English-speaking students of Chinese.

Printed in Great Britain
by Amazon